Post Traumatic Slavery Disorder

Definition, Diagnosis and Treatment

OMAR G. REID, PSY.D,

SEKOU MIMS, M.Ed MSW,

LARRY HIGGINBOTTOM, MSW, LCSW.

By
CONQUERING BOOKS, LLC
210 East Arrowhead Dr. #1 – Charlotte, N. C. 28213
(704) 509-2226 publish@conqueringbooks.com
www.conqueringbooks.com

SECOND EDITION - THIRD PRINTING
AUGUST 11, 2005

Library of Congress Number   2004093076
ISBN # 1-56411-373-6   YBBG#0369

Printed
In the
U. S. A.
By
CONQUERING BOOKS, LLC
210 East Arrowhead Dr. #1 – Charlotte, N. C. 28213
(704) 509-2226 publish@conqueringbooks.com
www.conqueringbooks.com

Distributed by
www.khabooks.com

Contents

CHAPTER 3

CHAPTER 4

Acknowledgments

All praises due to God, Allah, Jehovah, Ra, Yaweh, Buddha, and the other names that people assign the creator of all things. We also acknowledge the works, consultations, and teachings of Dr. Nai'm Akbar, Dr. Jawanza Kunjufu, the late Dr. Amos Wilson, Dr. Arthur Whaley, Dr. Ronald Fudge, Dr. Claude Anderson, Dr. Ivan Sertima, Dr. Virgil Woods, the late Elijah Muhammad, Minister Farrakhan, Minister Kevin Muhammad, Minister Don Muhammad, Dr. Asa Hilliard, Dr. Frances C. Welsing, Dr. Jacob Carruthers, Dr. Wade Nobles, Dr. James Comer, Dr. Alvin F. Poussaint, Dr. Joy DeGruy Leary, Donald Reid, Sr, Ann Reid, and the late Dr. Chancellor Williams and many others who have contributed to our understanding of *Post Traumatic Slavery Disorder*.

We thank our parents, immediate and extended family, ancestral family, and the Black community for giving us the support and the foundation to bring forth this needed information.

This book is dedicated to the late Reverend Mark Quitman Higginbottom, Sr., the late Ms. Mamie Mims, and her sister, the late Savannah Willams, and the late Frank Mack.

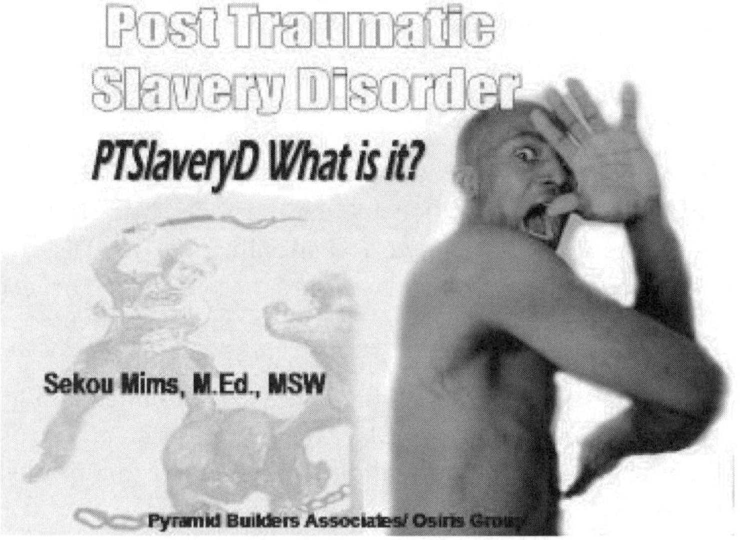
Post Traumatic
Slavery Disorder
PTSlaveryD What is it?
Sekou Mims, M.Ed., MSW
Pyramid Builders Associates/ Osiris Group

Introduction to Post Traumatic Slavery Disorder "PTSlaveryD"

"When you control a man's mind you don't have to worry about his actions. You do not have to tell him not to stand here or go yonder. He will automatically find his proper place and stay in it. You do not need to send him to the back door. He will go without being told. In fact, if there is no back door, he will cut one for his special benefit."

**Carter G. Woodson,
Miseducation of the Negro**

This book is designed to give readers an understanding of slavery's impact on and contribution to many of the dysfunctional behaviors exhibited by American Black people today. It is not about blaming Whites or about reparations, even though the information presented here supports the idea that Blacks have been damaged by both slavery and by "American Apartheid" (Jim Crow) laws.

The objective of this book is to offer participants **[readers]** a new clinical paradigm—Post Traumatic Slavery Disorder (the shorthand "PTSlaveryD" will be used throughout the rest of this work)—for working with Black people, whom my colleagues and I will usually refer to as Nubians[1]. The authors will illustrate how current dysfunctional behaviors and disorders that exist among Black people have origins linked to the African slave period. In addition, we will discuss the effects of the intergenerational transmission of the slavery trauma that is exhibited among Black people today from various social and economic classes. We will give readers information vital to help them identify the symptoms of PTSlaveryD in individuals, families, or groups. This book will also provide the participants with recommended strategies for treating this disorder. This book is intended for mental health clinicians, educators, and others interested in understanding the impact that the slavery experience has on Black people today.

Learning Objectives

1. To understand the origins of PtSlaveryD
2. To diagnose individuals suffering from PtSlaveryD
3. To identify the symptoms of PtSlaveryD
4. To be able to use an effective clinical approach to treat the disorder

---

[1]   Nubians are considered to include Black African Americans, Black Caribbean Americans, Black South-Americans, Afro-Latinos, and Cape Verdeans, who are the descendants of African slaves.

Sekou Mims, M.Ed. MSW

My mother was a strong Georgia-born Black woman with only a 4th grade education, one of 16 siblings. As a child, she witnessed the physical and economic lynching of strong-willed Black men and women. At the beginning of WWII, when she was 18, all of her brothers joined the military, and my mother and her sisters moved north to work in the factories.

After living in a number of cities, including Chicago and Detroit, my mother settled in New York in 1950. I was born in Brooklyn New York, but my siblings and I were raised in Boston in a single-parent household. We were very poor; I used to cut and shape cardboards in order to cover the holes in the soles of my shoes. I still have scars from frostbite on my hands and feet because of inadequate winter clothing.

My mother was very afraid for me. She told me that I possessed a very "strong will" (strong spirit). The childhood traumas and experiences that formed her while she was growing up in Georgia also provided her with a profound understanding of those dysfunctional Caucasian authority types who exhibited a widespread and obsessive resentment of Black Americans who presented then, and continue to present now, an indomitable spirit—especially Black males.

For Example: One of my elder cousins recently told me about an incident that occurred in Georgia when she was around 6 years old. She said that white men on horses came to her home in the middle of the night and attempted to lynch her father (my uncle Tot). As she told the story, I could see in her face the horror she had experienced. She was actually shaking. According to her, these white men told my uncle that he was an "uppity and arrogant nigger." Uncle Tot was a strong-willed Black Man!

My own experience confirmed that my mother's understanding was "on point" about many Caucasians' resentment of the descendants of former African slaves who dared to express any sense of pride and strength. Whenever I expressed or demonstrated my "spirit" as a child, I got into a lot of trouble with school officials and the institution known as the *criminal justice system*! I was labeled "aggressive and arrogant."

However, I was a very inquisitive and curious child. If I wanted to experience or learn about something, I would engage and indulge in whatever it was, regardless of the environment and the consequences. The consequences was usually either getting chased by peers and adults from other neighborhoods, or being arrested and brutalized by police officers.

The consequence I could expect to receive at home was a serious "ass whipping" (physical abuse) from my mother! I learned later that "ass whippings" were something the descendants of slaves had learned from slavery. *They literally learned how to discipline their children from the slave master.* Slaves often beat their children in order to protect them from the slave master. Unfortunately, slaves had to beat their children until the master was satisfied, but the slaves knew that they would not lose control as their masters often did. This practice of physical discipline continued well after slavery ended. Even as a child, I observed that there was a significant difference between how Northern parents and Southern-born parents disciplined their children: Southern parents were significantly more severe, my mother included.

My mother actually thought there was something seriously wrong with me because I would usually not cry when being whipped. I can count the number of times that I have cried in my life on one hand.

One of those few times occurred when, as a teenager, I read a book about atrocities that Africans experienced during the *African Holocaust* (a.k.a. slavery).

After reading that book, I broke down in tears. It described two specific atrocities that profoundly affected me. The first atrocity was how the slaves were brought to the slave breaking islands (Jamaica, Barbados, Cuba, etc.) and how the Caucasian slave enforcers (overseers) would gather together all of the pregnant African women. Then the overseers would randomly pick from one to 10 women (depending how many slaves had been captured) and hang them by their feet. An overseer would then take a machete and slice open the hanging women's abdomens, one by one, and they would force the other pregnant women to watch the un-born children fall out of the sliced women's wombs. The pregnant women who were forced to watch were also traumatized by this. In fact, some people believe that the trauma and fear they experienced while watching was immediately transmitted to their unborn children. I realize that I have believed, and continue to believe this as well. This belief is reflected in a saying I heard often while growing up: "Niggers are born scared."

The second atrocity that affected me so deeply described a common disciplinary practice that slave owners used when they caught African slave parents teaching their native language to their children. The overseers would cut the child into pieces and force the parent to watch as they fed the child's mutilated body to the hogs. Another "disciplinary practice" was to cut out the parents or child's tongue with a knife as though digging a clam out of its shell.

As I read the accounts of these atrocities, my mind developed vivid snapshots of them. I felt the horror and the helplessness of the victims and recalled a statement by the Honorable Elijah Muhammad: "If you knew 1/16 of what the Caucasian man did during slavery you would go mad overnight." These readings also reminded me of how hurt I was when my maternal grandmother died in 1962. I was the only sibling my mother didn't take to the funeral in Georgia. When I asked her why she didn't take me, she said, "Them white folks are not hurting my boy."

As a young man growing up on the urban streets of two major cities (New York City and Boston), I experienced several near-death situations resulting from confrontations with white authority figures. I spent most of my adolescent years in juvenile reformatories and adult penal systems, where (along with other children) I was brutalized by adult Caucasian men. While in those places, I would ask myself "Why are these grown men treating children this way?" I promised myself that some day I would put myself in a position to help young people who were compromised as I was then.

Early in my professional career, I worked in prison halfway houses, vocational programs, community centers, and DYS programs (Department of Youth Services— Massachussetts' criminal justice department for adolescents). But it was when I worked as a court clinician (Roxbury District Court, Boston, MA) that I realized I needed to develop formal clinical skills in order to work more effectively with the descendants of African slaves.

While employed at Roxbury District Court, I met Dr. Imani Wilson (a forensic clinical psychologist) and Bob Thornell (a licensed independent social worker and supervisor of the court clinic). They mentored me and convinced me that I could be more effective by combining my life experiences with formal clinical education. Four years later, I received a Masters Degree in Counseling/ Psychology from Cambridge College, where I learned how to articulate clinical strategies and effectively develop comprehensive treatment plans.

However, shortly after graduating with a M.Ed., I felt the need for more clinical education and I enrolled at Simmons School of Social Work, where I earned a Masters in Social Work. Simmons taught me how to combine clinical knowledge with research methods, which helped me to understand, justify and articulate in writing the need for more specialized interventions.

I also learned how environmental factors—i.e., family, social, cultural, occupational, community, economics and other non-specified conditions—can negatively or positively impact an individual. My Simmons experience also helped me to take a step further toward understanding that conditions that an individual experiences can not only impact their development, but that these conditions can also impact the development of a whole race of people. Clearly, Black and White Americans have had diametrically different experiences, *and the conditions to which they have been subjected have also been very different.* As a result, there are dramatic differences in their development and in their "worldviews."

After graduating from Simmons School of Social Work, I co-founded and now serve as the CEO of Pyramid Builders Associates, Inc. (PBA). PBA is an agency that employs Nubians and paraprofessionals who provide comprehensive Nubian-centric clinical and social services to communities in the greater Boston area.

I also provide consultative services to several mental health clinics, organizations, and agencies. I am a professional in the Psychology Department of the Boston Public Schools (BPS), where the services I provide include crisis intervention, individual and group counseling, home visits, and social assessments. I attend and participate in individual education program (IEP) meetings and am a member of the BPS *Trauma/Crisis Team.*

My clinical specialties include: trauma therapy, violence prevention, conflict resolution, substance abuse and anger management group counseling (specializing in the facilitation of all-male groups).

My co-authors also have many years of practical and clinical experience, and educational training. It is from this combined background, education and experience that we offer the definition of and proposed treatment for Post Traumatic Slavery Disorder(PTSlaveryD).

In order to effectively explain and define PTSlaveryD, we must briefly review the past 400 hundred year history of Nubian peoples. We are well aware that there are millions of Nubians who do not know their own history. For example, African-Americans ask me what do Puerto Ricans and Cape Verdeans have to do with being Black. Obviously, the people that ask the question don't know and understand that prior to the *African Holocaust there* was no such thing as an Afro-Puerto Rican, Dominican, Panamanian, Costa Ricans, Hondurans, Cubans, Brazilians, Cape Verdeans, Creoles or African-Caribbean Americans as they are known. *All of these delineations exist as a result of slavery.* The particulars that distinguish them include the countries where they were enslaved, the language they were forced to speak, and the cultures that they developed. Aside from these differences, they are people of the same African blood and rich heritage.

Facts About The African Holocaust

After the initial version of this PTSlaveryD manuscript was distributed, my co-authors and I participated in several interviews. These interviews consisted of TV and radio talk shows across America. We were also featured in several newspaper articles. It became perfectly clear that the majority of Americans, especially White Americans, neither know about and nor do they understand the atrocities that occurred during the African Holocaust. They also do not have a clue about the current impact that the African Holocaust has had on the descendants (Nubians) of the Africans who were subjected to the Holocaust/Diaspora. This widespread ignorance is due to the influence of Euro-America on the academic systems of the world, which have intentionally and systematically buried the "dirty secrets" of American history and its central role in the African Holocaust. What has been taught has been sparse. Rather than delve into the history of African slavery as has been done with other major world historical atrocities, academia has provided mere scraps of knowledge about the *African Holocaust* (slavery).

Euro-Americans and some Negro scholars have not even referred to, or acknowledged African slavery as a "Holocaust." Therefore, the average Caucasian person (as well as far too many Black persons) has been "bamboozled" regarding the whole truth about African slavery. For this reason, it is understandable to some degree why White Americans do not appropriately appreciate, understand and empathize with the *African Slave Holocaust/Diaspora,* but the situation goes much deeper than that.

It appears that the general consensus and questions among White Americans in regards to the African Holocaust is, "What is the big deal?" "I didn't have anything to do with slavery." "Why can't Black people stop thinking about slavery?" "Can't you people just move on?" White Americans have presented these questions to Black Americans for decades.

In all the radio talk shows in which we participated, a particular point and question was always asked. The question was: "slavery ended over 100 years ago. Why can't they just move on?" *This shows that the conscious thought of the majority of Americans is that the African Holocaust has no current relevance and should be forgotten.*

I never hear anyone say to the Jews: "The Jewish Holocaust happened over 60 years ago. Can't you people forget and move on?. Jews vowed to never forget and I don't believe that they should. What the Germans did to the Jews was a dark mark on history and should never be forgotten. Unfortunately, there appears to be a concerted effort to forget what was done to the African slaves during the African Holocaust. (*Note:* There has also been a concerted effort to ignore the Native American Holocaust. This country celebrates Christopher Columbus as a hero. Among some historians, however, it is believed that Columbus was responsible for the genocide and deaths of at least as many people/cultures in his conquests as Hitler was in his.)

Such reoccurring comments and questions led me to envision this scenario: A man is sitting on another man's chest and arms, continually punches his face, beats it to a pulp, and knocks him unconscious several times. Yet amazingly and to the beaten man's credit, he survives the vicious assault; he is somehow able to get to his feet and walk away, but with a limp. The victimizer has the audacity to blame the victim because he cannot stand straight. Later the victimizer says to the victim: "You need to forget about the beating and get yourself together so you can help me do to someone else what I did to you."

The scenario is ironic. If one looks at the history of America, African-Americans have always been instrumental in White Americans. conquests. African slaves fought hard in the French and American Revolutions. A Black man named Crispus Attucks was the first person to give his life in the American Revolution.

Sadly, Black Americans were also instrumental in the conquering of Native American nations and the implementation of genocidal practices and policies that were visited upon these first Americans. The X slaves (Buffalo Soldiers) played a major role in exterminating and relocating Native Americans who lived in the American West. Seminole Blacks were relocated from Florida and placed in what was then a part of Mexico, now known as Texas and New Mexico. The Seminoles were enrolled in the American Cavalry and participated in the campaign to murder Native Americans.

African-Americans fought in the Spanish-American war and were war heroes in both World War I and World War II. The Tuskegee Airmen protected White bomber pilots. Also in World War II, Black Marines participated in the Philippines campaign. The history of the Black Marines and the role they played in the South Pacific during WW II is still not mentioned in movies, media, and the history books that are written by Caucasian historians (*his story*).

Black Marines and paratroopers participated and died in the Korean War. Young Black male teenagers fought and died in the Vietnam War. Black soldiers were present in "Desert Storm I." Currently, un-told numbers of young Nubian-American solders are dying and being injured in Iraq and Afghanistan. There are Black James Bonds/special operations agents traveling around the world completing secret missions for their victimizers in the name of patriotism (jingoism.).

General Colin Powell appears to be jingoistic, but for some reason I have an emotional tie to, and respect for, him. Unfortunately, my respect for him is not consistent with my knowledge of him and his apparent jingoistic ideology.

About PTSlaveryD

It is no secret that mental health professionals are taught traditional European approaches and techniques in regards to mental health treatments. What has not been discussed frequently enough is that the Euro-American model only fits those for whom it was designed. The authors of this book (PBA) believe that a number of culturally relevant experiences from a wide variety of ethnic groups must be included with the globally known "traditional therapeutic approaches" Since our expertise is with those of the African Diaspora, we have focused our discussion on the ineffectiveness of traditional Euro-American mental health approaches in treating Nubians who are in need of mental health services.

It is necessary and paramount for mental health workers who work with Nubians to know the definition and have knowledge and understanding of PTSlaveryD. The traditional Euro-America's schools of social work and psychology have not adequately equipped mental health professionals of all ethnicities to provide effective mental health treatment to the descendants of the *African Holocaust.*

Is this failure to adequately prepare students and mental health professionals with the means to provide adequate and effective comprehensive mental health services for Nubians intentional or unintentional? That is a question the reader will have to research and answer. Nonetheless, it should be your goal as a mental health provider to provide the best services possible to all clients regardless of their ethnicity and background.

The word "background" is key to developing an Understanding of PTSlaveryD; it is used in reference to history. We believe that it is important first and foremost that Nubian mental health professionals know the history of the presented complaints, problems, issues and disorders that stem from the displacement (Diaspora) of Africans through the African Slave Trade so they can better help their clients and assist the affected communities to heal from the massive post trauma caused by the *African Holocaust.*

In order for medical doctors to effectively treat a medical problem or make an accurate diagnosis, they first need to hear the complaint and explore the medical background of the patient and explore the symptoms. When doctors explore a patient's history and symptoms, it increases their chances of developing an accurate diagnosis. Clinicians who are equipped with the appropriate diagnoses are able to develop an effective treatments. If a medical or mental health patient is wrongly diagnosed (mis-diagnosed), it is highly probable that the treatment plan will be inadequate and the patient's condition will not improve.

Traditional social work and psychology schools teach mental health professionals how to formally provide mental health services and research techniques. Mental health professionals who complete these academic programs are considered "qualified" to provide mental health therapy.

However, when we look at America's public schools, incarceration rate, rising rate of suicides, and the growing number of dysfunctional families that exist among both

White and Nubian-Americans, it seems only intelligent to break away from the traditional mental health disciplines and approaches.

Nubian-American clinicians must begin to think non-traditionally and independently in order to define the pathologies that have historically and continuously fractured Nubian-American's culture and communities. Nubian mental health professionals are in the best position to research their people's experiences, consult with other professionals, objectively test and sample other models, and use the best and the most effective comprehensive practices that will best serve their client population.

It is an absolute necessity for Nubian mental health professionals to develop curricula and clinical approaches that we know will work. We cannot wait for approval or validation from the traditional mental health establishment. We Nubians must define ourselves; we must move to the forefront and tell our own stories. Whenever a group depends on another group to define it, then that group will be molded to the specifications of the definer. Don't forget: America only recently deleted from its law books the notion that Nubians are only 3/5th of a human being.

Like many of you, we know what the problems are, and we have tried a variety of traditional techniques that proved unsuccessful.

As mental health professionals, my colleagues—Larry Higginbottom, MSW, LCSW, and Omar Reid, Psy.D,—and I understand that we have to define ourselves and our problems from a Nubian (Afro-centric) perspective. We have done just that with our research, definition, and approach to PTSlaveryD.

The vast majority of psychiatrists, psychologists, social workers, and mental health counselors practice the traditional Euro-American mental health approaches and treatments on Nubians because for the most part, they do not know any other treatment, nor do they appear to be interested in learning any others. It is evident to us that the traditional Euro-American mental health discipline is inherently biased and myopic. It views the mental health problems of descendants of the former African Slave as insignificant! Euro-centric practitioners will invariably "blame the victim" whenever it is suggested that racism or post-slavery conditions might be a cause of mental health disorder.

For example: When a client does not respond to a clinical mental health treatment, the tendency is for the clinician to categorize the client as resistant, oppositional and defiant.

Quite often when a Nubian male presents anger or some form of passive hostility he is derogatorily categorized and diagnosed with a neurotic or personality disorder. As a clinician, I would be worried if Nubian-Americans did not present some form of anger or hostilities after being subjected to 400 hundred years of Euro-centric insensitivity and oppositional diagnoses. If I met a Nubian whose affect did not appear negatively impacted due to the 400 years of degradation, I would most likely diagnose him or her with a neurotic disorder, one that describes a severely impaired affect (emotional numbing; self-induced amnesia; shame; guilt; and denial). It has been counter-productive and fruitless to apply the traditional Euro-American mental health model to Nubians, especially Nubian-Americans

With all the discord I have identified regarding the Euro-American traditional mental health model, it is ironic that Nubian-Americans are part of traditional America. Unfortunately, America's history of tradition has had a profoundly negative impact on the current descendants of the *African Holocaust.*

Both the way that Nubians were transported to the Americas (United States, Caribbean, and South America) and the brutality, exploitation and degradation they suffered was not only inhumane, it was very different from the way other immigrant groups were treated. However, many

European (White) Americans considered this mis-treatment normal and perfectly acceptable.

Other immigrants did not come close to experiencing the suffering, the brutality and the barbarism that Nubian-Americans endured at the hands of their former slave masters during slavery, which continued even after slavery was supposedly de-institutionalized. (America's systemic institutionalized *White Supremacy*).

Remember that America's indigenous people, the Native Americans, experienced a Holocaust similar to Nubian-Americans. It was similar with respect to the numbers of lives that were lost and the degradation the victims experienced. Millions of Native Americans were slaughtered. Currently, they are still experiencing the effects of the 400 to 500 years of continued subjection to brutality, degradation, subordination, and assimilation.

However, there are two distinct differences between the similarities of the Nubian American Holocaust and the Native American Holocaust. First, Nubians were forcibly transported to an unfamiliar foreign land, while America was the home of Native Americans. Native Americans at least had a "home field advantage" that allowed them the opportunity to defend and fight on their own turf. Their turf was where their culture was developed and maintained, while Africans lost the connection to their homeland and their culture. Second, the slave master gave specific Native American tribes ("the five civilized tribes") the "privilege" to own slaves. In fairness to the five tribes, the privilege was short-lived because they did not treat the African slaves in the manner the White Man wanted them to.

Yes, I acknowledge that several other ethnic groups were treated harshly, brutalized and suffered degradation upon their arrival and during their stay in America. Nonetheless, they were not enslaved, denied education, or murdered at the rate of African Americans, nor were they kept in bondage for 400 years. It strikes me as absurd when some people from other ethnic groups compare their experiences in this country and the suffering of their ancestors to the experiences of Nubian-Americans. In 2002, Dr Reid and I were guests on the CNN talk show *Talk Back Live*. A white audience member compared the loss of all her grandparents. money and fortune in the great depression to the experiences of Nubian-Americans, and asserted that because *they* had "dealt with it and moved on" so should Nubian-Americans. Her statement again highlights how ignorant most of the people in this country are to the history of slavery and how Nubian-Americans have been affected.

Once, on the Fox New Channel program *The O'Reilly Factor*, Bill O'Reilly (the show's host) compared the Irish migration and the harsh substandard treatment his ancestors endured at the hands of their cousins, the Anglo-Americans, to the 400 years experience of Nubian-Americans. He conveniently did not mention the fact that a very large percentage of the African slave overseers were Irish immigrants. He also did not mention the Irish-led race riot in 1863 that resulted in the murder of thousands of Black-Americans. My question to Mr. O. Reilly is: "Do you not have knowledge of the mentioned history or is it insignificant to you and not worth mentioning?"

These examples are further evidence that the American people in general have been bamboozled concerning the history of the *African Slave Holocaust*. In fact, history books do not present African slavery as a holocaust at all. It is commonly believed that, during the middle passage, 80 to 100 million Nubians lost their lives on their way to the Americas. That figure does not include the untold number of Nubians who were murdered and lynched physically, culturally, and economically after their arrival.

The fact that traditional Euro-American academia will not acknowledge and label African slavery as a holocaust that occurred in American history again raises the issue of what often appears to be the deliberate disregard for and misrepresentation of the African slavery experience by traditional Euro-centric academia. It is a glaring example of the kind of dishonesty that is the foundation of American history, which has been disseminated around the world.

It often appears as though the majority of Euro-Americans do not want to know the truth: that they do not want an accurate account of African slavery presented to the world. My colleagues and I believe that Euro-Americans know innately that there was a profound evil that manifested itself in the treatment of African slaves by Euro-Americans. The reasons for the "avoidance" of these facts are, of course, complicated and beyond the scope of this book. However, we believe that a major factor is that facing this truth could be psychologically devastating as it may challenge the sense of supremacy that Euro-Americans have been so indoctrinated to embrace. Facing the fact that slavery was indeed the *African Holocaust challenges the myth that America is always on the "right" side, and there are many for whom this realization could be overwhelming.* This is a classic case of mass denial and rationalization through indoctrination.

From elementary school to high school, I was always told and reminded by White teachers that African Kings sold Africans. This was presented as a form of rationalization of African slavery. I was even told by White teachers that slavery was good for Africans. In elementary school, several White teachers told me, "If we didn't come and get y'all, y'all would still be uncivilized and swinging from vines like monkeys."

In *Ego Psychology and Social Work Practice* by Eda G Goldstein (1984), Anna Freud, daughter of Sigmund Freud, describes the ego defense called "rationalization." According to Anna Freud, *"The mechanism of rationalization is the use of convincing reasons to justify certain ideas, feelings or actions so as to avoid recognizing their true underlying motive, which is unacceptable."*

Rationalization and denial are taught in Euro-American academia. Upon examining the indoctrination from a psychological standpoint, it becomes evident that this indoctrination was designed by the "powers that be" to maintain domination over the so-called Third World people and to protect the psyche of Caucasians. Denial is a defense designed to ward off shame and guilt in order to protect the ego.

White Americans present themselves to the world as the moral examples and arbiters of the world. They invade countries for doing what they do. They topple governments for possessing weapons that they possess. The United States develops laws for other nations to follow, and then breaks its own laws. *For example:* the United States participated in developing the international law that it is a violation of international law for a country to assassinate a head of a state, yet the United States regularly seeks to assassinate heads of states both covertly and overtly. The United States continues to deny its own illegal and immoral behavior and consistently projects its own behavior onto that of other nations. During and after slavery, White males consistently presented the propaganda that Nubian males wanted to rape and ravage White women, yet the rape of Nubian women by White men was commonly accepted.

During the early part of the 20th Century, it was common knowledge among Nubian-Americans that the majority of Nubian men who were lynched and murdered for raping white women had not committed the crimes. White males, with the complicit knowledge of the victims, law officers, and the community-at-large, committed the majority of the rapes.

This example is a clear case of mass "projection." To this day, Caucasians continue to project their own dysfunctional psyche, deficiencies and behaviors, as defined by Euro-Centric mental health models, onto Nubians.

This book was not designed to point out the Caucasian people's psychological deficiencies or assign blame. It was developed to focus on some of the Nubian-Americans current psychological deficiencies and accurately define them. This task could not be done without accurately pointing out some historical and present day facts. It was not developed to support the cause for reparations, although we believe that some form of reparations to Nubian-Americans is warranted. This book was designed as a tool for all clinicians of all ethnicities. It was also developed for the average Nubian person as an aide for understanding the confusion and conflicting feelings they see in themselves, their loved ones, and their people.

We have heard several Caucasians and Nubians say that we are looking for excuses. We ask in return, "Excuses for what?" When clinicians of other races and ethnic groups provide services for their clients, they are not looking for an excuse. They are trying to assist their clients to resolve or appropriately cope with the presented problems or complaints.

Jewish clinicians who provide therapeutic services to Jewish clients who have been affected directly or indirectly by the Holocaust are not looking for excuses. They know from where the problems stem. They know the mass trauma that their people experienced. Their work is centered on assisting their clients to develop solutions and effective coping skills. Why it is that when Nubians write and speak about the Nubian Holocaust, Caucasians become defensive and quite often take offense?

A typical response is to down play the Nubian Holocaust experience by suggesting that the descendants of the African slaves have not actually suffered the carnage of slavery, so why all of the fuss? We will show in this book that what happened during slavery continues to have an effect on the descendants of slaves. Considering what Nubians have been through in America, we have made tremendous strides, accomplishments and contributions from which everyone has benefited, and continues to benefit from today. But these accomplishments do not mitigate the effects of slavery.

The authors are researchers, healers and social scientists who understand the universal laws of nature. One law that we completely understand is the law that everything that exists has a beginning and a history. That history may vary from 5 seconds to millions of years. Problems are not exempt from laws. We understand that everything has a route. We also understand that tangible and non-tangible things have a tendency to appear to evolve endlessly. Sometimes the process of evolving may require assistance.

The problems of Nubian-Americans are not exempt from the laws of beginning/history and evolving/escalation. We will show how the psychological problems of Nubian-Americans were initiated and have evolved with assistance. In the next sections we will show how mass trauma evolved into PTSlaveryD.

An Overview of PTSlaveryD

TRANS-NATIONAL TRAVEL: It is estimated that more than 80,000,000 Africans lost their lives during transport through the middle passage from Africa to America. However, it is almost impossible to estimate the number of slaves that lost their lives during bondage in the Americas and other countries due to the absence of record keeping. While the loss of life was one of the greatest human traumas in any history, the African Holocaust is one that few have acknowledged or talked about in mental health arenas.

Scholars have attempted to estimate the number Africans who lost their lives in the "middle passage" by comparing the estimated African population before slavery, particularly the African countries involved in the slave trade, to the estimated population after the transportation of slaves was outlawed and the estimated number of slaves who existed in the Americas. Unfortunately, there is no way of obtaining an accurate count.

Some readers may ask, "What does the *African Holocaust* have to do with providing therapy, and what was the objective of developing the PTSlaveryD diagnosis?" We hope that we have shed some light on the topic thus far. Nonetheless, we will examine the opinions of other mental health professionals.

In his book *Breaking the Chains of Psychological Slavery* (1997), Na'im Akbar explains the importance of understanding the magnitude of the African slave's trauma:

> "The objective is to identify the magnitude of the slave trauma and suggest the persistence of a post-slavery traumatic stress syndrome, which still affects the African-American personality. It is not a call to vindicate the cause of the condition, but to challenge Black people to recognize the symptom of the condition and master it as we have mastered the original trauma . . . . It is to call attention to an array of attitudes, habits and behaviors, which clearly follow a direct lineage to slavery. It is the hope that, by shining the light of awareness on these recesses of our past, we can begin to conquer the ghosts which continue to haunt our personal and social lives."

Our goal is not to re-traumatize Nubians. Our goal is to un-traumatize ("de-niggerize".) We want to undo slavery's negative impact. We want to break the chains of slavery that currently exist in Nubian people. Once PTSlaveryD is recognized by Nubians, it can automatically become one of the mechanisms that will help undo some of the negative effects of the 400 years of madness that Nubians to which have been subjected.

We are aware that the descendants of the *African Holocaust* do not like to be reminded of the horrors of their slave history. It is common knowledge among clinicians that trauma victims do not like to be reminded of the trauma that they experienced, especially in the initial stages of therapy. It is common for trauma victims to avoid anything that reminds them of their traumatic experience. The *Diagnostic Statistical Manuel 4th Edition* (DSM IV) explains that avoidance is one of the symptoms of Posttraumatic Stress Disorder (PTSD). It has generally been my experience that when I talk about the history of the *African Holocaust* with the descendants of African slaves, the majority of them will say, "I don't want to hear that slave 'shit'! Can't we just move on?" I usually reply, "Yes, but not until we get rid of the shackles that are impairing our ability to move on successfully." We must face the past in order to rid ourselves of our current issues.

This section will be very brief because the majority of us know something about *African-slave history.* American schools equate "Black history" with "slave history," even though Nubians are the oldest people on this planet, whose history did not begin in America. Nubians built the pyramids and created math and science, yet American schools have successfully perpetuated the myth that Nubians have only been "civilized" for 400 to 500 years (slave history). According to history taught in most American schools, prior to slavery, Nubians were considered by Whites to be "jungle bunnies" swinging on vines, climbing trees, and "uncivilized." Africa has never been presented in American schools as what it truly is: The cradle of all civilization. No wonder profound numbers of Nubian-American youths have low self-esteem!

These facts should make it crystal clear to the attentive reader that the vast majority of Caucasians and Nubians have no understanding of how the atrocities that were committed in the *African Holocaust* continue to impact Nubians psychologically, socially, and economically.

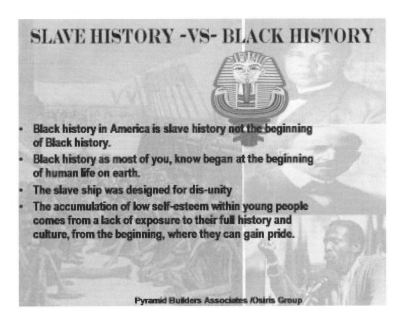

SLAVE HISTORY -VS- BLACK HISTORY

* Black history in America is slave history not the beginning of Black history.
* Black history as most of you, know began at the beginning of human life on earth.
* The slave ship was designed for dis-unity
* The accumulation of low self-esteem within young people comes from a lack of exposure to their full history and culture, from the beginning, where they can gain pride.

Pyramid Builders Associates /Osiris Group

The History

First, let us make something perfectly clear. No one went to Africa, shot Africans with guns, slapped them on their backs with whips, and then enslaved them without encountering courageous resistance from the Africans. Turning Africans into slaves was a difficult undertaking that led to decades, and even centuries, of war between Africans, Europeans, and Arabs.

From the very beginning of the slave industry, Africans resisted capture and fought vigorously and violently. There were untold numbers of battles in which slaves took command of slave ships and killed their captors. Many slave ships floated back to Europe from Africa with all of their crew dead. The threat of enslavement caused many Africans to flee their homelands to avoid capture. Resistance included individual, family and tribal suicides.

In America, organized slave rebellions resulted in widespread loss of life for many slave owners and their entire families. Thousands of run-away slaves settled in the American West before Lewis & Clark's journeys. Many African slaves fought against their subjugation by resorting to "passive-aggressive" forms of rebellion. However, slave-owners overcame slave resistance by becoming more brutal and inhumane in their efforts to subjugate African slaves through mass lynchings, mutilations, and other atrocities.

In 1812 the great Nat Turner, a preacher and slave, initiated a slave rebellion in Virginia that has echoed down the generations. Nat Turner's rebellion was one of the largest recorded slave revolts in the history of North America, which started in Virginia and spread through the Carolinas.

The African-slave institution and all the slave doctrines that followed gained greater acceptance with the end of the slave rebellions.

One notable historical example demonstrates the development of the African-slave institution (the making of a "nigger") and the doctrines that were developed to quell the "rebellious spirit" of the Nubian. In 1712, Virginia slave owners invited long-time slave owner and consultant Willie Lynch, who lived in the West Indies, to consult with and teach them how to control their slaves.

As a well-known expert on slave control, Mr. Lynch wrote several letters outlining how to develop ultimate control over

African slaves. Lynch taught Virginia slave masters several brutal psychological techniques to use in the interests of control and economics. I will point out just a few key techniques that Willie Lynch prescribed.

In *The Making of a Slave* (1999), Lushina Book has documented some of the Willie Lynch letters for readers who want to know more. Portions of some of the letters are given below:

Males: "Take the meanest and most restless nigger, strip him of his clothes in front of the remaining male niggers, the female, and the nigger infant, tar and feather him, tie each leg to a different horse in opposite directions, set him a fire and beat both horses to pull him apart in front of the remaining niggers."

The next step is to take a bullwhip and beat another nigger male to the point of death in front of the female and the infant. Don't kill him."

Females: "Take a female, run a series of tests on her to see if she will submit to your desires willingly. Test her in every way because she is the most important factor of good economics. If she shows any signs of resistance in submitting completely to your will, do not hesitate to use the bullwhip on her to extract the last bit of bitch out of her. Take care not to kill her, for in doing so you spoil good economics. When in complete submission, she will train her off-spring in the early years to submit to labor when they come of age."

Family: "We breed two nigger males with two nigger females. Then we take the nigger males from them and keep them moving and working. Say the one nigger female bears a nigger female and the other bears a nigger male. Both nigger females being without the influence of a nigger image, frozen with an independent psychology, will raise their offspring into reverse positions. The one with the female offspring will teach her to be like herself. The one with the nigger male offspring, she being frozen with a subconscious fear for life, will raise him to be mentally dependent and weak, but physically strong. Now in a few years when these two offspring become fertile for early reproduction, we will mate and breed others like them to continue the cycle. That is good, sound, and long range comprehensive planning."

Controlled Language: "We must completely annihilate the mother tongue to both the new nigger and the new mule and institute a new language that involves the new life's work of both. You know language is a particular institution. It leads to the heart of a people. For example, you take a slave, if you teach him all about your language, he will know all your secrets, and he is then no more a slave, for you can't fool him any longer, and being a fool is one of the basic ingredients of and incidents to the maintenance of the slavery system."

Psychological impact of the loss of History: "By reversing the position of the male and the female savages, we have created an orbiting cycle that turns on its own axis forever . . . Our experts warned us about the possibility of this phenomenon occurring, for they say the mind has a strong drive to correct and re-correct a period of time if it can touch substantial original historical base. They advise us the best way to deal with the phenomenon is to shave off the brute's mental history and create a multiplicity of phenomena of illusions that each illusion will twirl in its own orbit, something similar to floating balls in a vacuum."

Children: "A brief discourse in an offspring development will shed light on the key to sound economic principles. Pay little attention in the generation of original breaking but concentrate on future generations."

Willie Lynch assured Virginia slave owners that if they followed his instructions they would obtain complete control for centuries. It is difficult not to be startled when one reads his assertion that the use of his techniques would insure they could "not only control current slaves, but all future generations." The key words that stood out to me while examining Lunch's instructions and interpreting his letters were: psychological, fools, frozen, eminence, orbit, generations, recycling and forever.

As you can see, American slave owners *deliberately acted to* de-humanize and relegate African slaves to an inferior status known as "niggers." There was a concentrated effort to institutionalize the practice of *recycling niggers.* Surely this evidence is proof that America's slave owners were *at least* as venal as those Nazis who conspired to subjugate and eliminate Jews during what is commonly called the "Jewish Holocaust."

The terrorism that slave masters inflicted on African slaves devolved into psychological trauma that was *meant to be* transmitted from generation to generation. This psychological trauma has negatively impacted the psyches of slave descendants for successive generations. These inter-generational affects developed into a psychological snowball that has rolled uninterrupted for centuries. *The psychological snowball has devolved into a present day avalanche of several psychological and physical disorders* that continue to exist among the descendants of the *African Holocaust.*

In the "Intergenerational Handbook of Multigenerational Legacies of Trauma," edited by Yael Danieli, Michaels (1958) refers to testimonies and findings regarding the inter-generational effects of trauma:

> *"Holocaust Testimonies at Yale University we have found that knowledge of psychic trauma weaves through the memories of several generations, marking those who know of it as secret bearers.*

> *Furthermore, we have found that massive trauma*
> *has an amorphous presence not defined by place*
> *or time and lacking a beginning, middle, or end,*
> *and that it shapes the internal representation of*
> *reality of several generations, becoming an*
> *unconscious organizing principle passed on by*
> *parents and internalized by their children".*
> *"Traumatic memory thus entails a process of*
> *evolution that requires several generations in which*
> *to play itself out (Laub & Auerhahn, 1984)."*

These findings appear to be "on point." We also understand that it may take several generations for traumatic memories to play themselves out. However, what if the populations of the people that have experienced a catastrophic traumatic event (such as slavery) continue to be traumatized? What is the extent of the evolution of the trauma memories? Is there a continued evolving of the "amorphous presence"? These are questions that readers may be able to better answer after reading this book and eventually other social scientists will also accurately answer.

Our contention is that the psychic trauma that weaved through the inter-generational memories of the descendants of the African slaves has resulted in the present day phenomenon of PTSlaveryD.

Posttraumatic Stress Disorder or PTSlaveryD

PTSlaveryD is not described in the *Diagnostic and Statistical Manuel Of Mental Disorders 4th Edition* (DSM-IV). PTSlaveryD is a non-traditional diagnosis that was developed and defined by the founders of Pyramid Builders Associates, Inc. (PBA). PTSlaveryD emerged as a relative and comparative diagnosis of the hundreds of clients seen across our mental health spectrum.

Based on our client success rate, PBA decided to create this book/manual for mental health clinicians and other human service professionals to use when addressing specific issues that are encompassed by PTSlaveryD. As we work our way through the book, we will compare and contrast the traditional PTSD diagnosis with PTSlaveryD.

The Need for the Definition PTSlaveryD

The next section compares and contrasts "PTSlaveryD" with PTSD and briefly shows the comparative disorders of PTSlaveryD. We will demonstrate some of the observed modalities, responses, and behaviors that clearly exist in the descendants of the *"African Holocaust."* This section concludes with the question, "Has PTSlaveryD played out and evolved into a chronic condition that can be labeled Chronic Traumatic Slavery Disorder (CTSD)?"

This section explains and demonstrates the current toxicity and the pathology of PTSlaveryD and its development into what we have come to believe is a chronicity of PTSlaveryD among the Nubian population. We will also explain some of the modalities that have evolved due to the chronicity of PTSlaveryD, such as mental suicide and mental homicide (*Mentalcide*). The definition of PTSlaveryD is based on the behaviors that Black people have developed in response to the initial trauma of slavery.

By publishing this book, we hope our readers will come to understand the urgent need to facilitate and implement an intervention program based on these findings. The illustrations may appear simple, but they are very effective. In order for mental health professionals to effectively digest, understand and apply the techniques suggested here, we recommend that they should first apply them to themselves. Consistency is the key to applying the interventions & preventive strategies that Dr. Reid articulates. We believe that a large-scale implementation of these suggestions will be the beginning of a cure for the mass pathology of PTSlaveryD.

In the final section, Dr. Reid's anecdotal approach to treating the symptoms and the modalities of PTSlaveryD was written with a view to it becoming a global approach.

It appears that Nubians are on the threshold of losing their grip on their collective spirit, identity, mind, and soul. This author remembers a commercial that used to play on a local Black radio show, which stated, "They can take our music but, they can't take our soul." Nubians appear to be dangerously close to losing their collective souls. How do we begin to reinforce our grip on our identity? At Pyramid Builders, the authors have found that the feelings of loss are due to the several disorders that have been developed over the 400 to 500 years of slavery, followed by "Jim Crowism" and the on- going fight for peripheral inclusion in democracy.

What has been most difficult to overcome is that after so many years of non-Nubians defining Nubians, the negative and degrading advertising and propaganda about Nubians continues to be so effective that everyone, Nubians included, buys into the negative definitions and stereotypes. Nubians have been assigned to and assimilated into the negative roles. It is as if they were given a script and are playing the role.

Nubians' dysfunctions have been and continue to be defined from a Euro-American perspective. However, as previously stated, we understand that after what Nubians have been subjected to for 400 to 500 years, it would be impossible for them not to have been negatively impacted as a mass of people. Nonetheless, we argue that neither

Nubian people nor their required treatment modalities should continue to be defined by the Euro-American academic mental health approaches.

If this practice of defining what is best for Nubians from a Euro-American perspective continues, the descendants of the former African slaves will continue to not receive appropriate mental health treatment, but will remain dysfunctional in the eyes of the world and themselves. In effect, they will continue to be victimized.

Both Euro-American academic institutions and the U.S. government defined Nubians as 3/5 of a human being. That doctrine was recently removed, under protest. Therefore, the motives of "powers that be" are purely about maintaining power and control, which enhances their ego and increases their need to maintain the institutions of *White Supremacy.* The institutions of power include public schools, colleges and universities, the judicial system, financial institutions, government and medical—particularly mental health-institutions. These institutions define everyone and control their levels of functioning in society; therefore, it can be demonstrated that the mentioned institutions also control the levels of poverty and dysfunction, as well as the regulation and distribution of empowerment information.

Information is the key that opens the locked doors of the institutions of power. As a race, Black people have been in the position to receive empowerment information from academic institutions. However, they were not taught to recognize power or how to use it to benefit their people, even though they posses every type of academic degree from institutions of higher learning. Therefore, the techniques we present are designed to empower Nubians.

According to the late Amos N. Wilson (1993), "If our education is not about gaining real power, we are being mis-educated and misled and we will die educated and misled."

We have interpreted Dr. Wilson and other Nubian scholars and writers who appear to have similar ideology to mean that the intention of Euro-American academic institutions is not to empower Nubian people, but to control them by developing Nubians into efficient servants, better overseers and "high income house slaves."

Nubian educators, writers and producers are in the best position to tell Nubian people's stories, just as Nubian social workers and psychologists are in the best position to define and treat their peoples. dysfunctions and illnesses. However, Nubian professionals must first understand what illnesses and dysfunctions befall them as well as their students, audiences, clients and patients. Nubian professionals must develop an "Afro-centric" (Nubian perspective) point of view and approach. They must observe and listen to themselves as well as their clientele. They must listen, examine and understand the history of what has happened to the descendants of the former slaves and use this information to develop culturally-competent interventions and treatment modalities.

By doing this, they will develop the ability to understand the inefficiencies of the current tools, such as the DSM IV, to define people. They will be able to compare and contrast, as we did, the traditional PTSD and non-traditional PTSlaveryD.

Next is a brief example comparing and contrasting PTSD and PTSlaveryD. Let's look at what is relative.

Posttraumatic Stress Disorder

Posttraumatic Stress Disorder (PTSD) is described in the *Diagnostic and Statistical Manual four* (DSM-IV). In fact, insurance companies will not reimburse independent practices or health management organizations (HMO) with out DSM IV diagnoses. The DSM-IV is the primary tool used by mental health clinicians for relative and comparative diagnoses. The latest version of the Diagnostic *Statistical Manual* is the DSM-IV, the fourth edition.

According to Criterion A2 of the DSM-IV, the essential feature of Post Traumatic Stress Disorder is the development of characteristic symptoms following exposure to an extreme traumatic stressor with direct personal experience of an event that involves actual or threatened death, serious injury, other threat to one's physical integrity; witnessing an event that involves death, a threat to the physical integrity of another person, learning about unexpected or violent death, serious harm, threat of death or injury experienced by a family member or other close associate.

Symptoms

- Criterion A2 states that the person's response to the event must involve intense fear, helplessness, or horror (or in children, the response must involve disorganized or agitated behavior).
- Criterion B of the DSM IV requires that characteristic symptoms resulting from exposure to the extreme trauma include persistent re-experiencing of the traumatic event.
- Criterion C describes the persistent avoidance of stimuli associated with the trauma and numbing of general responsiveness.
- Criterion D describes persistent symptoms of increased arousal.
- Criterion E states that the full symptom picture must be present for more than one month.
- Criterion F states that the disturbance must cause clinically significant distress or impairment in social, occupational, or other important areas of functioning.

DSM-IV Defined Specifiers :

Acute: The duration is less than 3 months.

Chronic: The symptoms have lasted 3 months or longer.

With delayed Onset: At least 6 months have passed between The traumatic event and the onset of the symptoms.

Pyramid Builders Associates

Carlson (1997) provides a very straightforward table of responses of PTSD. The table is as follows:

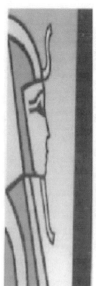

DSM-IV Defined Specifiers :

Carlson (1997) provides a very straight forward table of response of PTSD. The Table is as follows:

Mode	Re-experiencing	Avoidance
Cognitive	Intrusive thoughts Intrusive Images	Amnesia of Trauma Derealization /Depersonalization
Affective	Anxiety Anger	Emotional Numbing Isolation Affect
Behavioral	Increased activity Aggression	Avoidance of Trauma Related situations
Physiological	Physiological Reactivity to Trauma Reminders	Sensory Numbing
Multiple Modes	Flashbacks Nightmares	Complex Activities In Dissociated States

Pyramid Builders Associates

Reaction/Results/Responses

Effects on the Individual
- Substance Abuse
- Violence
- Low Self-Esteem
- Fear of Individualism
- Avoidance
- Identity
- Schizoid Character
- Spiritual Blocks

Effects on the Family
- Minimal Participation
- Breakup of the family
- Loss of income/culture
- Recurring abuse/violence

Secondary and Associated Responses:

Carlson (1997) also points to secondary responses to trauma.

- Depression
- Aggression
- Low Self-Esteem
- Identity Crisis
- Problems with Interpersonal Relationships
- Guilt and Shame

Associated Disorders:

"There may be increased risk of Panic Disorder, Agoraphobia, Obsessive-Compulsive disorder, and Substance-Related disorders. It is not known to what extent these disorders preceded or follows the onset of Post Traumatic Stress Disorder."

The DSM-IV has shortcomings. For one thing, it does not reflect cultural differences. *For example*: there is nothing in the DSM-IV that reflects any diagnosis that is caused by **racism**. Some experts would dispute the diagnosis of racism or the associated pathologies and disorders that are caused by racism.

For instance, this author had a 14-year old client who was 6 foot four, 235 lbs., with almost "blue black" skin color. His teeth shone like white pearls and his hair was jet black. He was a very handsome young fellow. However, he was experiencing extreme anger, low self-esteem, and was at the beginning stage of developing a paranoid disorder. His chief complaints were that he couldn't walk down the street or play basketball without the police searching him, molesting him (feeling his genitals) and disrespecting him. Occasionally, the police would even beat him. He said to me he did not understand why police who did not know him would ride by and look at him like they hated him. He also complained that he could not go in a store without being followed, disrespected and even kicked out because they did not want him there. He told me that when he was 12, he went into a store, walked-up to the Latino male counter person, and the man pulled out a and aimed a shotgun at him. My client told me he did not understand why this man feared him. He said all he wanted to do was to buy an ice cream cone. This young man further explained that his schoolteachers, both black and white, treated him like he is different than everybody else and that that they have always treated him as an adult. He further explained that his family also treats him differently because he is the darkest person in his family). He expressed that he does not feel secure and does not like the color of his skin, which is due to the negative blatant and subliminal images associated with being a dark complexioned black.

Another example for the need for the diagnosis of Racism:

I also had a 40 year-old Nubian-American client who appeared to be experiencing symptoms due to racism. Born in Alabama, she was the second youngest of five siblings (three brothers and one sister) and was the darkest of all her siblings. As a child, she was continually teased by her family members and peers due to her dark skin. She said that her lighter skinned sister was always considered the "good one" and that schoolteachers also appeared to be partial to the lighter skinned children. Teachers expressed low expectations of her. She expressed that she experienced low self-esteem as a child. When she was 14, a friend of her elder brother raped her and her family's response was, "What did you do?" She became pregnant due to the rape. At age 18, she moved to Boston with her daughter, where she earned a pretty good living and worked at several jobs. Several of her friends and associates were white, including her best friend, who was a colleague and White woman her age. She explained to me that she was happy then and an easy-going person. But one day her best friend and colleague called her a "nigger" and, in her words, she "flipped out." She apparently blacked out, yet found a letter opener and sliced her friend several times. As result, her friend received over 90 stitches and almost lost her eye and my client served two years in prison.

I formally met this woman several years after her release from prison. She presented as a 40-year-old disorganized person who didn't know what was next. After I examined her history, it was apparent that all of her disorders and symptoms were the result of racism from other Blacks and White people. She was severely traumatized due to racism and other life events. From the initial traumas, several associated disorders followed, including: Agoraphobia (fear of crowds), Obsessive Compulsive Disorder (particular issues associated with lack of impulse control), Major Depression and Post Traumatic Stress Disorder. She also experienced several features of PTSD. All these disorders could have been put under the diagnostic PTSD umbrella. Some of them did not fully manifest or become apparent for decades.

Currently, this woman is doing very well. She is self-employed, own a car (prior to treatment, she was scared to drive), and does not demonstrate any fear of crowds. She also appears to be task oriented, to have gained better control of her impulses, and to not become overly obsessed to the point that it impairs her ability to perform other tasks.

This was only accomplished after two years of treatment, which consisted initially of weekly individual counseling sessions that eventual diminished to monthly counseling sessions. The treatment was also combined with limited pharmacological treatment. It would not been successful if I had not gained clear knowledge of her trauma history and also her people's trauma history (Nubian people), especially with respect to the intra-racial prejudice that is prevalent among Black people due to the slavery experience.

Clinical Definition of PTSlaveryD

While working for the Boston Public Schools (BPS), the author received a psychological assessment on a new student. The person who prepared the assessment was a Caucasian female psychologist who worked as a consultant for BPS. In the assessment, she concluded that the young Nubian male in question was experiencing several diagnoses, including: borderline personality disorder, interment explosive disorder, posttraumatic stress disorder, and major depression.

After assessing the young man myself, I agreed that the diagnosis of PTSD associated with major depression was appropriate. I later called the psychologist and asked her on what basis she had made the diagnoses of borderline personality disorder and intermittent explosive disorder. During the conversation, I pointed out to her that diagnosing a student under 18 with a personality disorder was totally incorrect due to his age, and that intermittent explosive disorder appeared to be unfounded to me. I explained to her that all of the associated diagnoses could fall under the umbrella of PTSD and would be less stigmatizing. She immediately agreed to amend her psychological assessment. However, while she agreed to amend her assessment, she was also very arrogant. She did not express any regret and was somewhat resistant. In fact, she initially would not talk to me until she was assured that I was a Master's level clinician. After my experience with her, I asked myself how many other Nubian students she had misdiagnosed and what her predisposition or general perception of Nubian males might be. This story is an important example because, in a nutshell, it defines the ease with which Nubian children are routinely misdiagnosed and demonized. This misdiagnosing of Black children has a profound effect on their future lives.

The development of PTSlaveryD demands that mental health professionals revisit not only the definitions and labeling that our clients have to live with, but also examine our own relationship with and perception to these definitions and clients.

We will begin to examine a clinical definition of PTSlaveryD by asking a series of questions: "Why do we need a new definition for Post Traumatic Stress Disorder that specifically relates to Nubian people? What impact does PTSlaveryD have on other descendants of African slaves (Afro-Caribbean, Afro-Latinos, Afro-Brazilians, Afro-Cape Verdean's and Afro-Europeans), and what are the similarities with the descendants of the American Diaspora? What is the pathology of *Post Traumatic slavery Disorder*? What are the similarities between PTSlaveryD & PTSD? Why is a PTSlaveryD curriculum needed in the profession of *mental health*?

As previously explained, PTSD stems from a traumatic event. The African slavery/Diaspora was a massive traumatic event. Competent clinicians understand that shortly after a traumatic event occurs, it is important to immediately acknowledge it and to intervene with the victims through clinical debriefings in order to minimize the negative impact and future ramifications.

The primary technique a clinician uses depends on his or her observations and the collection of data (record of chief complaints). An open-minded clinician can see that Nubian people as a whole are experiencing the symptoms of PTSD in direct relation to the traumas of the *"African Holocaust,"* and some more then others. Let's look at how the symptoms relate to Nubian people.

Avoidance: Avoidance is a defense mechanism that assists an individual to minimize feelings that cause discomfort and trigger negative modalities. The average descendant of slaves does not like to be reminded of slavery; instead, they find themselves avoiding reminders of slavery such as dialogue, reading materials and documentaries. Avoidance occurs within Nubian people of all classes, professions, and educational backgrounds.

I find myself avoiding films on African slavery because they profoundly anger me. Because I am well versed on ancient African history, I also experience feelings of resentment because African slave history is presented as if it is the only history of Nubian Americans. Nubian history is presented as if it started on the onset of African slavery! However, the history of African slavery is very relative and is an important part of Nubians. history. Slavery is why they currently live in the Americas. Prior to slavery, there were no Puerto Ricans (Latinos), Cape Verdeans, Haitians, Jamaicans, African Americans, Creoles etc.

Identity: Trauma victims are often known to adopt their victimizer's identity. *For example*: molestation victims have been known to develop into perpetrators themselves. Male children who witness domestic abuse are at higher risk of becoming abusers. During chattel slavery, when the master was absent, the slave who was left in charge usually acted like the master. In most cases, he was just as abusive to his fellow slaves as was his master. This behavior has been observed in present-day Nubian police officers, bank officials, administrators, mental health workers, etc. Black people have been taught to hate themselves and anything associated with being black. This is why it is easy for a Nubian person to kill someone who looks like him or her. This self-hatred is also why Nubian people are preoccupied with changing their appearance. The change is normally directed to look as much like the descendants of the slave masters as possible. Many Nubians are preoccupied with the texture of their hair, shape of their noses and lips and the shade of their skin (e.g., Michael Jackson).

There are skin color sayings that exist among Nubian Americans stemming from slavery. *For example:* "If you light you're alright, if your brown stick around, and if you're Black get back." When I was a child, when a Nubian American male described a beautiful Nubian woman she was normally light skin and her hair was considered good hair because it was either straight or close to it. It was rare when a dark skinned woman was associated with being beautiful.

When I was an adolescent, a Nubian girl who was braiding my hair said, "You may be dark but at least you have good hair." Nubian children grow up thinking that everything associated with being black is negative or has negative underlying connotations.

For example: the bad family member is the "**black sheep**" of the family. If a **black cat** crosses your path, it's bad luck. Bad magic is "**black magic**." The clothes worn in heaven are portrayed as white, versus the clothes worn in hell that are portrayed as black. Angel food cake is white versus chocolate devil food cake. In cowboy movies, the good guy's had is **white** and the bad guy's hat is **black**. When a person is using information against you, it is called **"black mail."** When an individual is banned from a profession or an organized social club, it is called being **"blackballed."** When the stock market crashed in the 1920's, it was labeled **"Black Tuesday."**

A child—Black or White—who grows up bombarded with such negative blatant and subliminal messages as those mentioned can develop a negative attitude towards the color black and anything associated with it. Maybe that is why, when a Nubian child is born the parents, relative and friends are preoccupied with the child's skin color and the hair texture. The baby could have 52 toes and no one will take notice prior to their preoccupation with the child's skin color and hair texture.

Recently, the author watched a news program that showed a yearly Columbian custom. The custom was that Columbia annually has an ugly person contest. The story showed that some people in the crowd grabbed a very dark-skinned Nubian-Columbian and made him get on the stage and proclaimed him the winner. You could see the shame, fear and discomfort on his face.

I once interviewed the mother of one of my clients. My client was a very beautiful, 14 year-old Nubian-Puerto Rican girl. The mother was what Nubians would consider golden brown. As the mother continued with the interview, she stated where my client inherited her good looks, explaining that she has a sister who is very light skinned. She told me about an incident that occurred when she was child. She was walking down the street with her mother and a woman approached them and said to her mother, "you have such a beautiful daughter." Her mother replied, "You should see my other daughter". I could see the pain that this woman had experienced from what her mother said. She then told me I was the first person to whom she ever told that story, which occurred 30 years ago.

More negative subliminal suggestions: In football, the head referee wears a white hat, his subordinates wear a black hat with white stripes. When police shoot at black images when they do target practice. Even police dogs are affected by negative subliminal suggestions. Police dogs are normally trained by using black and dark objects. In the game of pool, the chief ball, the cue ball, is white. The object of the game is to use the cue ball to knock the opponent's balls off the table, with the goal to kill the black ball. In Black churches,. pictures Jesus portray Him as a Caucasian man (Michael Angelo's cousin), when it is commonly believed that Jesus is a man of color. The world of Christian theology has not attempted to replace the portrait of Jesus with an accurate portrait. During the Christian Crusades, which was the onset of White Supremacy, there was a considerable effort to destroy all accurate images of Jesus, but that is another story. The world of theology assumes it would be psychologically catastrophic to White Supremacy if the real image of Jesus was presented, that their egos would fragment overnight and that White Supremacy would lose control of their people and their subordinates. Further explanation of this type of dogma is slated for another book of discussion.

Interpersonal Relationships: Interpersonal relationships are impaired by identity issues and self-hatred. It is difficult for individuals to love others if they don't know how to love themselves. Remember that during slavery, there was a concentrated effort by the master to destroy the Nubian family. Many argue that the separation of the Nubian family was continued after slavery through the welfare system. The man was not allowed to live at home with his family so the woman and her children could receive assistance.

Emotional Numbing: Slaves were forced to watch their offspring being brutalized, disrespected, and sold. Relationships among the slaves were encouraged only for the purpose of breeding them. It was not feasible for the male slaves to develop an emotional attachment to their offspring. When attachments developed, they usually were short lived due to the children being sold and Black men not having any family control. Currently, Nubian males continue to have difficulty connecting emotionally to their children and women.

Isolation of Affect: Nubian clinicians are taught that showing affection to their clients goes against the grain of the Euro-American style of clinical discipline. Many of these clinicians therefore have a reputation of not being able to relate to their clients. They fear that they may not meet their boss's approval and won't fit in and as a result, they become very disengaged.

Anger: Nubian people have demonstrated their anger more commonly by reacting to difficult incidents with acts of violence or self-destruction rather than with legal action. Normally, an event that triggers a mass demonstration of anger unleashes accumulated aggression. This is why we have seen Nubians demonstrate mass anger in the form of spontaneous explosions, which are usually an un-organized outbreak of expressions *For example:* The historic Chicago fires after the destruction of the Black Panther Party, the violent mob scenes after the murder of Dr. Martin Luther King and/or the Beating of Rodney King are some recent examples.

All PTSlaveryD symptoms impair an individual's behavior and responses, as well as their everyday perceptions. Historically, Nubian people's behavior and their general perceptions have been impaired and distorted, and they continue to be distorted because of a lack of treatment was caused by the traumas of slavery and the years following the emancipation. As a result of slavery and the continual inflicted traumas inherent in the exploitation of capitalism in all of its forms (racism, sexism, and religious bigotry), the symptoms of PTSlaveryD have become chronic. The chronicity of PTSlaveryD raises the question "Has PTSlaveryD developed in *Chronic Traumatic Stress Disorder?*"

Psychotic Disorders: Black people experience several psychotic disorders. When one of the author's sons was 16, he went through what is called "brief psychotic disorder."

He presented both visual and auditory delusional symptoms and expressed suicidal ideations. His chief complaint was racism. I remember saying to myself that my son has not experienced 1/10 of the overt racism that I have, so why is racism affecting him to such an extent?

During his psychotic episode, I spoke to a colleague who was completing his psychology practicum at Boston Medical Center. He explained that young African-American and Afro-Latino males were being referred for counseling in high numbers and many presented with the same complaint as my son's. I realized that my son might be re-experiencing not only my experiences, but my father and mother's experiences, and so on. I was seeing the uninterrupted snowball effect of slavery and the American apartheid manifested in my home.

I have facilitated several groups for males aged 5-50. Several of the adult groups comprised prisoners, ex-prisoners, or others mandated by the courts. However, whether they were ex-prisoners or not, the thing that all male group participants had in common were: 1) They were predominantly Black and Afro-Latino males. 2) They were angry. The most common theme was, "I don't know where this anger, nervousness, anxiety, and sadness are coming from."

This author has also worked with several professional Black clients who were financially well off. All of them expressed confusion about their depression, anxiety and anger. Even though they were re-traumatized by a variety of personal events, they expressed feelings of confusion and ignorance about the onset of these symptoms and asked why they were experiencing them. Several have said to me, "What do I have to be angry about?"

The reader should see a common thread in the psychological experiences of Nubians, regardless of their social class. In closing, it is clear that to this present day, the trauma of the greatest holocaust known in the history of man has never been fully acknowledged. There have never been any organized interventions or debriefings. Usually, the descendants of the former slave masters and the former slaves all avoid the discussion of slavery, though obviously for different reasons. One reason that both the magnitude and the realization of the atrocities are too horrific to conceptualize in any spiritual value system currently known to conscious man. It is hard for individuals to present righteousness if they know they are a descendant of evil. One would have to lie to himself.

Normally, present day White Americans hang their hats on not being responsible for the *African Holocaust,* although they still benefit economically from it. Instead, they blame it on their ancestors. However, White Supremacy is responsible for continuing the mechanisms that continue to traumatize Black people, including academia, economic institutions, mental health institutions, medical institutions and the government. They are making sure that the snowball continues to roll. This book has three sections. In chapter 1 we offered a brief history of the *African Holocaust* (slavery) and a brief explanation of PTSD and PTSlaveryD as they relate to the *"African Holocaust."* With this as a foundation, we can now begin to discuss and define post-slavery trauma and its effect on the descendants of the **African Holocaust**. In Chapter 2 we travel briefly through the civil rights movement in America and explain the comparative trauma of "Jim Crowism" and "Economic Terrorism," which have led to the traumatization that continues to negatively impact the descendants of the **African Holocaust**. In chapters 3 and 4, Dr. Reid will define the healthy mind, body and spirit and will outline interventions and strategiesfor practitioners who work with those who suffer from PTSlaveryD.

My colleague, Larry Higginbottom, MSW, LCSW, founder of the Osiris Group, will in the next chapter describe the impact of PTSlavery D on Black people today.

Shattering the Veil of Mental Homicide & Suicide "Mentalcide"

A person's ability to capitalize on their own knowledge, information and learning comes from a healthy mental state of being. When a person has a healthy mental state of being they are able to think clearly, coherently and independently on behalf of their own personal development as well as that of their family and community.

According to Webster's Dictionary, the word culture has a variety of meanings in several categories. For the purpose of this text the term culture is used with the following interpretation: 5a The integrated pattern of human knowledge, belief and behavior that depends upon personal capacity for learning and transmitting knowledge to succeeding generations. 5b The customary beliefs, social forms, and material traits of a racial, religious or social group; And 5c The set of shared attitudes, values, goals and practices that characterize a company, corporation or people.

With that said, I would like to add, even a masters degree and/or cultural sensitivity training will not qualify a culturally incompetent individual to be effective in a position of power over students, professionals, or others whom they do not understand.

About the Author

Larry Higginbottom, MSW, LCSW

Since 1991, I have had the good fortune to meet Black professionals who work in virtually every sector of social services. Through these meetings, I have become very knowledgeable about the internal workings of The Department of Social Services, Department of Youth Services, the Juvenile Courts, The Boston Public Schools, the Community and Mental Health Centers, Transitional Social Services, and the Boys & Girls Clubs to name a few.

From 1984 to 1986, prior to entering the field of social services, I was employed as a registered representative for First Investors, stock brokerage house. During my two years there I advised clients on appropriate investment strategies to meet their personal needs. In June 1986, I transferred to Dean Witter Reynolds, where as a stock broker I offered clients timely investments strategies to meet their needs. What I remember most about the stock brokering experience is that *"results"* had no color or gender preference. Those who understood the business climate and could translate that knowledge into a language which the investor understood and felt comfortable with over the phone, where the individuals who would close more sales. I did not possess the gift. I was merely average over the phone, so it would not have been a wise decision for Dean Witter to put me into a position of authority or leadership.

In 1988, just before I exited this results driven industry, I worked with Prudential Financial Services for two years and while I enjoyed it—I needed to replace my commissioned income with a steady salary after my first and only child, a daughter, was born in 1991. As I examined potential career options a friend from college who had just accepted a position as Director of the Mattahunt Community Center in Boston, MA, suggested that I interview for the position of Program Director. I was offered the position with a start date of July 5 1991. The first thing I began to notice immediately was the differences between the corporate and non-profit cultures. The corporate culture, having a bottom-line driven mandate, was proficient and efficient in its service delivery. However in the public sector this was not necessarily the case. It was quite commonplace in the public sector to follow a directive that all parties agreed *did not work*, did not produce the desired results but, met funding needs. Another major difference was very clear in the corporate sector, as I alluded to earlier those who were designing investment strategies had proven that they understood the business climate and had demonstrated the ability to put that knowledge into a language that potential investors understood. And in the public sector it was strange to see the power that people had, without any culturally relevant experiences. People "in authority" were unable to put customs, cultures, values and norms into a comprehensive intervention strategy. And these "authorities" were designing and developing strategies for populations they had no community ties to so they had no fear of repercussion.

In my position, at the Mattahunt Community Center, I designed and implemented youth programs and trained staff to run them. My first observation at the Mattahunt was chaos. The children had no boundaries and the staff had no way of controlling them. My first forty-eight hours on the job were spent sitting and observing the lack of structure in programs, language etiquette, correct behavior, sexual norms, employee protocol; and in addition there were no mechanisms in place to hold the parents responsible for their child(rens) behavior. I realized that I had to be the beacon of integrity, boundaries and consequences. My first order of business was to give clear, distinct, boundaries (in third grade language that any adult or child could understand) to the staff and the children.

My second order of business was to make sure that when those new protocols were violated that the consequences were swift and certain. What I then experienced was a choosing of sides, those who wanted order yet thrived on chaos, and those who welcomed the boundaries and now could be more proficient. Those who really wanted chaos were written up and eventually terminated; and those who desperately needed order thrived. Additionally, the parents were brought into a partnership with the Mattahunt Community Center where they were made totally aware of the language and behavior that their child was engaged in once they left home (at times verbatim).

In January 1995, I was again summoned by my dear friend who had moved on to the Boys & Girls Clubs of Boston's Roxbury Clubhouse. He invited me to come and clean up the Roxbury Clubhouse based on our successes at the Mattahunt. And because we had faced the same situation and challenges, I now had a well timed methodology which could be calculated procedurally in the terms "six months to clean house." By September of 1996, things were running smoothly at the Roxbury Clubhouse, and I decided to enroll in Simmons College of Social Work to pursue a Masters Degree. While at Simmons, I accepted an internship with the Boston Department of Social Services (DSS) where I was assigned child abuse, child neglect and family disintegration cases. For the most part, I had to investigate a targeted person's family members, school personnel, etc. to get a sense of whether the claims were legitimate or not. What I learned from that process was when I went into homes, if I brought my definition of what normalcy and appropriate living conditions were, I made the mistake of superimposing my beliefs on the client rather than helping them with their real issues. It is a finite point but a pivotal one. The idea is not to become focused on the lack of physical or materialistic elements in their space (a four legged coffee table supported by three legs and a stack of books), but to stay focused on the issue bringing DSS there. such as a child left unattended.

By May 1998, I graduated with a Masters degree in Clinical Social Work. I had already determined the social sector I wanted to practice my craft in was the school system, so I sent my resume to the Boston Public Schools, the Newton Public Schools, and the Needham Public Schools. During the month of June I received calls for interviews from Newton and Needham (upper middle class suburban school systems). The interviews sent well at both institutions, and I was offered a second interview with the Newton Public School system.

Although I did not receive a second interview from the Needham Public School, the comments the caller made to my wife showed the importance that upper middle class (presumably Caucasian) decision makers place on staffing their social/educational institution with culturally competent professionals, namely themselves. The message left was as follows; "We (the committee) find that Mr. Higginbottom has some excellent skills, which could be of better use serving the youths of Boston."

Before you judge that statement consider this, I was forty-five at the time, had lived in Boston's neighborhood Roxbury all my life, knew nothing about affluent middle class ideology.

Additionally, I had worked at a community center and a Boys & Girls Club which caters to children from inner city neighborhoods, and all I had which qualified me for a position as clinician was a recently acquired masters degree, and the desire to care about people.

Was I qualified to work in the Newton Public School system? No! But if the situation were reversed where a naïve suburbanite came to work with the Boston Public School system, would the answer be yes? This is what urban professionals are forced to accept every working day, culturally unqualified, mostly Caucasian, individuals in charge of institutions that service primarily Black and Brown people.

Finally, in September 1998, I was offered a position in the Boston Public Schools. Lab Cluster at Brighton Public High School. And being newly authenticated with my degree in back pocket, after having learned all about Sigmund Freud, I was ready to apply *my* recently acquired middle-class repertoire on urban youth. The initial interventions I used included reframing, individual therapy, group therapy, point systems, level systems, behavior modification, and mediation. The students. sent to me were engaged in defiant, rude, oppositional and disrespectful behavior. The whole experience was a cultural disaster. I realized I had hit bottom when a female student was returned to me after we had a lengthy session of "alternative communication." She looked me in the eye, put her hand on her hip, waived her finger back and forth, and with her head waving from side to side announced: "Mr. Higginbottom, Caroline does what Caroline wants to do and there ain't _hit you or nobody else can do about it!. Believe it or not, a calmness came over my entire being and I quietly said to her, "You're right." I then went into my office and sat down, and took my DSM4 along with Sigmund Freud, put them both in the bottom drawer and closed it.

The first question I had to ask myself was, "If I had not gone to this prestigious college would I have used these methods of intervention for this anti-social behavior?" My answer was no! The second question I asked myself was, "Are these kids mentally or psychologically ill?" The answer was no. My final question was, "Within the broadness of all of my personal and professional experience, what would I call the behavior of these children?" The answer was just plain rude and disrespectful because these children placed no value on education.

So for the next several months I went into an observational mode, asking the children what they were doing with no books, no papers and so on, coming from communities so far away. Their responses ranged from, "All my friends are here," and "My mother won't let me stay home;" to "What the _uck is it to you!"

I concluded two things were important to these kids, a) mobility throughout the school, and b) socializing with their friends. So I decided to create a new model called "The Learning Center" based on three principals: 1) Refocus students on learning and not on peripheral classroom behavior; 2) Make freedom of movement and socializing a privilege and not a right; and 3) Make students regulate their own behavior, in a way that was classroom acceptable.

I gathered the cooperation of a few colleagues who were just as frustrated, and we created a classroom where ill behaved students could be sent to complete their work. Once in the Learning Center, if a student's work was not completed and if they did not self-regulate their behavior, they would stay an additional day, and so-on. Our rate of success was determined by the plummeting of in-classroom disruptions. What is important about what I have just shared is the cultural relevance that lended itself toward the solution, which I will try to further explain.

Omar G. Reid, Psy.D, Sekou Mims, M.Ed MSW, Larry Higginbottom, MSW, LCSW.

The Blanket of Misdiagnoses

According to the 1999 Federal Department of Education guidelines, students are classified for Special Education if they are diagnosed with the following : Autism, deafness, mental retardation, hearing impaired, speech impaired, visually impaired, orthopedically impaired, emotionally disturbed or learning disabled.

In the 1997-98 study conducted by John Verre from Compass consulting, there were 13,713 students in Special Education in the Boston Public Schools (BPS)and 1,039 students in the Lab-Cluster programs totaling 14,752 students out of the total BPS population of 63,762. This meant that 23.14% (or about 1 out of four) of the total student body of the Boston Public Schools were in Special Education programs.

Those numbers shocked me into reading a number of more recent BPS student case histories, from both the Lab Cluster and Special Education programs at Brighton High School. I then compared what I found with the case histories of mainstream, and "drop out" students at Brighton High. I was stunned when I found that approximately eighty-five percent (85%) of those students were diagnosed as either being "Emotionally Disturbed" or "Learning Disabled."

The 1999, Department of Education Federal Register defines the context of the term "Emotionally Disturbed" in the following manner:

(A) An inability to learn that cannot be explained by intellectual, sensory, or health factors.

(B) An inability to build or maintain satisfactory interpersonal relationships with peers and teachers.

(C) Inappropriate types of behavior or feelings under normal circumstances.

(D) A general pervasive mood of unhappiness or depression.

(E) A tendency to develop physical symptoms or fears associated with personal or school problems.

    (ii)   The term includes schizophrenia.

    (iii) The term does not apply to children, who are socially maladjusted, unless it is determined that they have an emotional disturbance.

These facts sent me on a mission over the next two years to read as many case studies as I could. After comparing hundreds of case histories from students who were then attending Brighton High School (as well as those who dropped out) with these Federal Guidelines, virtually *none* of the students who were referred into the Lab Cluster exhibited characteristics outlined in the federal guideline.

However, all of those students did fit under a rather loose umbrella of being "Emotionally Disturbed." The term Emotionally Disturbed for nearly eighty-five (85%) percent of one urban city high school's student body that was predominantly Black and Brown didn't sit right with me. So I began to analyze the *initial* cause for each student's referral into the Lab Cluster. What actually emerged was a portrait of most students exhibiting socially maladjusted behavior.

There are no federal or state guidelines for "Socially Maladjusted. behavior, however, all of these socially maladjusted students' narratives were identical, with virtually the same symptoms:

a) Regular use of profanities, cursing out teachers and peers;

b) Argumentative, constant talking, disruptive, disrespectful, rude;

c) Walking out of class, non-studious behavior;

d) Preventing teacher from teaching, many teacher/parent meetings;

e) Disturbing other students, being un-prepared for class;
f) Causing fights, threatening teachers or peers, physically striking teacher;
g) Many detentions, many suspensions etc.

What these symptoms actually revealed are two phenomena:

1. The lack of correct parental instruction; and
2. The school systems inability to construct a corrective apparatus to respond to the socially maladjusted student.

Other forms of misdiagnoses that designated students to Special Education and the Lab Cluster included classifying a student as Learning Disabled.

Putting aside childish things, A six-year-old girl awaits arrest.

Photo from "Why We Can't Wait", Dr. Martin Luther King, Jr.

A Time to Take A Stand

WEB DuBois	Booker T. Washington

If we reach back in history for a moment to reconcile our position; we can look to W.E.B. Dubois, who called individuals trained in college the "Talented Tenth." Dubois recognized that the race must have trained minds that can create and design solutions to our collective problems.

However, somewhere along the journey the "Talented Tenth" believed it was more advantageous to assimilate than to create the institutions to bring about a positive self-identity for our people. Dubois. Talented Tenth talks often include discourse about the mental shape the masses are in. I believe that we are going to have transform some of the processes within our respective institutions to help the masses. What about the other ninety percent?.

On one hand we are seen by our ancestors such as WEB Dubois as the "Talented Tenth," with a great responsibility to our people. On the other hand we are still seen as animals, a veil that has been created to exploit a great people by using slavery to justify capitalism.

"Mentalcide" 383 Years in the Making

While it is an acceptable fact that Africans were in the America's long before Columbus sailed for the new world; for the purpose of this discussion, we are going to begin our time period around 1619. This was when the boom in the mass importation of African's grew the institution of slavery. As Sekou has so clearly pointed out, the first stage in transforming an African tribal member into a slave was to keep him from thinking freely Which is the beginnings of "Mentalcide" that is Mental Homicide. That meant African people could no longer interact with their families and friends using their language(s), customs, values, norms, beliefs, rituals etc. That period lasted from 1619 until approximately 1865, or 246 years.

The second developmental stage of "Mentalcide," occurred from 1865 until about 1965, or what I have come to refer as (US Apartheid) the Jim Crow laws and the Black Codes, lasted another 100 years. The environment Blacks were confronted with when the legalization of slavery ended did not end the process of a developing social "Mentalcide," it caused a festering and growth.

Defining Mentalcide
Destruction of Our Own Self-Development

1619-1865	246 Years	Slave Conditioning
1865-1965	100 Years	Apartheid Jim Crowism
1965-2004	39 Years	Inclusion in Democracy

"Mentalcide" will develop when an individual has been estranged from thinking clearly, coherntly and independently due to extreme psychological, physical and emotional violence. Prolonged exposure to these conditions will also produce an alienation to knowledge, information or learning.

A woman is arrested during a peaceful demonstration march in Montgomery Alabama "Why We Can't Wait," Dr. Martin Luther King, Jr.

Who among us has not seen photos of angry white crowds standing around watching a disfigured black male on fire or hanging from a tree? Who among us has not heard the stories our grand parents told of whites cutting off ears, fingers or the organs of a black person? During that hundred years of terrorism it was commonplace for black females to lose their virginity through individual or gang rape by Caucasian males. This behavior in its truest form is derived from a psychological veil over the eyes of Caucasians that allowed them to see Blacks as animals. The veil we call "Mentalcide" turned human beings against their fellow human beings.

"Mentalcide" has three modalities as we understand it. 1) a brainwashing that allows one human being to abuse another mildly or extremely; 2) a visualization by one human being seeing different human beings as other than human; 3) and an effort on behalf of human beings to become something other than who they are to protect themselves. "Mentalcide" is traced throughout our arrival in America under the soul-less system of slavery, where some 80,000,000 lives were lost over 246 years—however, scholars argue that the one-hundred years after was the most violent.

During slavery, Blacks were afforded some degree of protection—after all Blacks were viewed as an article of commerce and this free labor was instrumental in producing wealth for the owner. After legal slavery ended, it became open season on Blacks by anyone considered Caucasian from ex-master to poor laborer, *anyone*. How many of you have heard or read about a Black person (male or female) who was assaulted or hanged because a Caucasian stated the Black person "sassed" them, was "acting uppity", "to big for his pants," or "that nigger thought he was smart." We all are aware that blacks were restricted to certain types of employment, had to enter places of employment through back door or the kitchen, had water fountains and bathrooms marked "Negro," and were not allowed to look at or walk on sidewalks with Caucasians. We should all know that during these times, Blacks could not live where they wanted to and anything they owned (from land to personal property) could be taken by any Caucasian so inclined. Recent records show that Black Americans owned 15 million acres of farmland in 1910, nearly all of it in the South. And during a 91 year period, 1910-2001, it was found that Blacks were powerless to prevent their decline in land ownership. Black men saw others lynched for whistling at white women and didn't dare challenge Caucasian authorities for stealing their land. Black landownership in the South today is down to about 1.1 million acres. During this one-hundred year period of mental and physical terrorism, mentioning equality, integration or the desire to have quality education for our children would get you shot, lynched, severely beaten or run out of town if you were Black.

So what type of mental and emotional perspective and/or personality gets developed in an individual who learns that irrespective of opportunity, it "need not apply" to them? Denial of the significance of the insult and/or suppression of the emotions it produces became the strategy to survive, the underpinnings of mental homicide and mental suicide, "Mentalcide."

After World War II, when it became apparent that the rights Blacks who fought and died on behalf of the world were not given to them in the "Land of the Free and the Home of the Brave." A movement of conscious resistance and defiance evolved and persisted among Blacks which spread among the masses. This conscious resistance found expression in a variety of historic events such as the Montgomery Bus Boycott and the famous college student sit-ins at Woolworth's and other businesses. Blacks held rallies, demonstrations; they marched onto city halls, defiant and angry, yet they peacefully demanded their rights to sit at the table of American life.

"Mentalcide" as Mental Homicide

What it will take for us to comprehend that the primary function of slavery was to transform the minds and personalities of the entire African race into a soulless article of commerce for the sole purpose capitalist exploitation? Now that slavery is over, we are dealing with a transformation process from emancipation and the Jim Crow laws during which "Mentalcide" emerged.

Mentalcide affects everyone! "Mentalcide" as mental homicide is the most obvious disorder under the umbrella of Post Traumatic Slavery Disorder. Mental homicide is what happens when a persons mind is controlled to the extent that he or she cannot see what is in front of their eyes. It is as though a veil has covered their eyes and they can only see what is on the veil. The afflicted person believes what they see to the extent that he will kill another to justify the veil. The act of killing another because of this veil is we have deemed mental homicide.

The essence of terror or fear tactics is to debilitate or immobilize a human spirit so that it cannot take protective or corrective measures from an aggressor. It is hope by the individual, the group or the race, which initiate this type of action that the victim will be so incapacitated with terror and fear they will surrender to the assault. The implicit message being implied is, I am all-powerful and only I can help you enjoy your life; here on earth I am God to you.

Have Blacks ever received messages and images from the Caucasian community which said to them loud and clear that you need to developed your mental intellect because the city of Boston, New York, Texas or these United States needs your mental creativity to help run it? As I thought back to my adolescent and teenage years about the messages and images which are marketed directly to black youth from the larger community: competing for power and influence was never part of the message.

"Mentalcide" as Mental Suicide

Mentalcide: a Conceptual Reference
A Veil Created by Slavery and Transferred from Generation to Generation by Institutions of Mass Media

- Institutions to control the image of the black race via stereotypes, many have not changed in 300 years, chattel images are still in place effecting us today.

- 22-year-old Amadou Diallo, described by his family as a devout Muslim who had never been in trouble with the law, died in February, 1999 in a hail of 41 bullets fired by 4 white police officers while he stood in his own doorway.

Those who are the targets of mental homicide understand what it is they are experiencing, although they have no psychological interpretation. In order to defend themselves from those who maintain and perpetuate the veil, they make themselves as small as possible, as insignificant as they can, as un-intimidating as they know how. These acts are the beginning of mental suicide. In order for a tall/large, brilliant, Black man to become small, insignificant and un-intimidating he will smoke, drink, do drugs, dress down, hunch his shoulders, be unkempt, and be uneducated. A striking, Black woman become insignificant by dressing and acting like a sexual object rather than a competitive person. This behavior begins in school, just around fourth grade.

I have written this text to carefully share my thoughts and views on this most difficult topic. How do I begin to ask you to deal with the aftermath of the institution of slavery? By 1965, we saw on television, one-hundred years of physical and emotional terrorism coming to an end. It was the signing of Civil Rights Bill, inclusion and equality was here at last. Or was it? We have learned at Pyramid Builders and Osiris Group that inclusion and equality are not an overnight thing. Tremendous physical, emotional, spiritual and intellectual damage has been done to an entire culture of people. With only 39 years of inclusion in democracy, a national healing has begun to take place; a healing from economic exclusion, a healing from recognition of the veil. Blacks are people not animals!

However, people all over the world have been subjected to a mental frame of reference about black people based on two-hundred and forty six years of slave conditioning, one hundred years of Apartheid/Jim Crowism, and thirty nine years of inclusion in democracy. The vision of Blacks as chattel/animals, the commercialization of Blacks as "Toms, Coons, Mulattoes, Mammies & Bucks," as Donald Bogle's book is named, will not go away without directed effort at replacing those images.

Omar G. Reid, Psy.D, Sekou Mims, M.Ed MSW, Larry Higginbottom, MSW, LCSW.

Shattering the Veil of "Mentalcide"

"Mentalcide" has developed as a result of an entire society having been estranged from thinking clearly, coherently and independently. Prolonged exposure to this mind control has produced an alienation to knowledge, information, or learning about the truth of the African Diaspora and Black people and culture.

Today's black clinicians are trying to bring wholeness, wellness and saneness to a process, which had a life span of three hundred eighty three years as the most extreme treatment recorded by the human species. To help, we have focused this chapter on defining the specifics of the problems that stem from the physical, emotional, spiritual and intellectual damage of an entire culture of people. In order to be effective in the process of healing our neighbors, our community and our people, we must first recognize our own issues and begin to heal ourselves. It is my hope black mental health providers will come to recognize the origins of "Mentalcide," and how these issues of our past are affecting our collective present and future. As clinicians we must bring consciousness to the clients we service in our communities.

For instance, how do we make it plain to see that the concept or practice in our males as it relates to fathering without obligation or commitment to the mother or the child originates in slavery? We have to convey the important functions which fathers normally provide: teacher, mentor, role model, counselor, disciplinarian, provider and protector. And we have to help them through their "Mentalcide" (mental suicide) toward internalization of a new paradigm in the idea of "man." We now know that terror and fear immobilizes and incapacitates an individual from selecting life giving/ saving options. We have all seen young brothers preferring not to be educated, not wanting to stand out. I have seen many of our bright male students prefer to play the role of the dummy, rather than excel academically, even though they knew what the outcome of their life would be. I have had many conversations with these young men and have asked, "Why are you choosing to fail?" The standard response is "If I wanted to pass I could, but I don't want to."

Economic Terrorism

The number one threat preventing black professionals from standing on integrity, honesty and truthfulness is economic terrorism: I define economic terrorism as follows: "Economic terrorism is defined as the perceived/verbalized or written threat of loss of income. It can also come in the form of the perception or anticipation of a ruined or derailed career, and/or the destruction of one's reputation or credibility." Economic terrorism has the same psychological and emotional effect as racial profiling, it's an affront against human rights, economic rights, and professional training. A legacy of terror and fear grips the minds of the professional, embedded in the psyche. Look at those gifted, talented, committed, professionally trained and culturally competent Blacks just collecting a check and waiting to retire. Are we content with just getting paid? Did we pursue our degrees to become order takers or administrators?

Economic terrorism denies the ideas, talents, and wisdom of individuals who are silenced and/or parked in their jobs. I have met many black professionals who paid a professional price when they had the courage to say, "This strategy will not work, or that strategy has failed." But other Black professionals who watch on the sidelines as our brothers and sisters who take a stand are subjected to economic terrorism have to live with their decision(s). Economic terror is when we are compelled not to join the ranks of those who are right because we fear for our own paycheck.

I believe it is our destiny as black professionals to challenge the practice of economic terrorism, because to many gifted brothers and sisters are being silenced and ruined because healthy and fair dissent or opposition is being oppressed; we need these creative people to fulfill their destiny. The black community needs our leadership and wisdom, as well as the white community does we all will win if we lead.

START YOUR OWN

The year 2065 will mark the one-hundredth anniversary of Black people's full inclusion in democracy. Will it find us still fighting individuals who practice economic terrorism or will we develop on a larger scale our own schools, social agencies, private practices, clinics, and recreation centers to develop the human spirit?

In order for civil, social and economic justice to prevail in America every generation of Black people has had to pick up the cross of oppression and carry it. Well it's our turn now to follow in that long tradition called resistance. I had no role in removing the actual chains from my flesh, but God sent Nat Turner, Harriet Tubman, Frederick Douglas and William Monroe Trotter. I had no role in eliminating brothers and sisters from being lynched, but God sent the brothers and sisters who joined and fought along with the NAACP. And finally I had no role to play in 1967, at The National Convention of Social Workers when a group of Black social workers walked out to form what has become the National Association of Black Social Workers. Why did these people take such measures? Black people's needs were not being met, and it's up to professionals like us to improve the living conditions for all of our people.

In the field of human and social services, a leadership and power structure has developed that is just the opposite of the population these sectors service. Most of our clientele (approximately 85 %) are Black and Brown, yet the individuals with authority and power are primarily middle class white suburbanites. The results of an elite suburban "authority" setting the agenda for education, prevention and/ or interventions with inner-city youths have had dismal to mediocre results at best. Surely those individuals currently in positions of "authority" do not posses the gift.

Post Traumatic Slavery Disorder (PTSlaveryD): Diagnosis and Treatment. A guide for Clinicians who work with Black people. Omar G. Reid, Psy.D.

> *"You did not land on Plymouth Rock. Plymouth Rock landed on you. You have been had, hoodwinked, bamboozled, and believe you are in a clear state of mind."*
>
> *Malcolm X*

The behavioral definition for Post Trauma Slavery Disorder (PTSlaveryD) and the African slave experience lies rooted within the veil of misperception. A group or person can only operate according to what they perceive. When Black children are born in this country their destiny is predetermined by the societal pathways they are allowed to access as well as from the impact that the effects of the multigenerational transmission of trauma has had on their family line. The individual affected by PTSlaveryD is conditioned through television, the ignorance of parents, family, community, the neglect of public school systems, wayward peers, and the transgenerational transmission of trauma to exist in an often deviant or sub par manner. PTSlaveryD is a cumulative effect of the slavery experience. It causes a paralysis of the psyche, body, and spirit. PTSslaveryD is mis-education, poor living, and eating habits that leads to countless medical problems and diseases. PTSlaveryD is a lack of self-history, and 'Mentalcide' (mental suicide and mental homicide). PTSlaveryD is a cancer that has been produced, enhanced, and maintained by the institutions that utilize capitalism to exploit the masses of Black people in the United States for economic gain. PTSlaveryD is not about reparations or blaming Whites for the condition of Black people today. PTSlaveryD is about helping those that work with the descendants of slaves to get a better understanding of how to effectively address their current issues that have roots back to the plantation. PTSlaveryD is not a new phenomena. *The international Handbook of Multigenerational Legacies of Trauma* (1998) is a must read book that gives empirical evidence of how the effects of trauma are passed from one generation to another in various cultural and ethnic groups.

Detoxification from PTSlaveryD

The previous writers in this book have revealed how this process of PTSlaveryD is manifested and maintained today. Therefore, to detox the individual or group from this disease, there must be a reconditioning of the mind, body, and spirit. This detoxification must involve a process of recovery that liberates any mind that has been conditioned to be enslaved. Detoxification requires, as Minister Kevin Muhammad, of the Nation of Islam in New York states, "mental surgery". Mental surgery is an operation involving a series of complex *incisions of knowledge,* which must be placed in the mind as the contaminated thought processes are being removed. Herman (1992) explains "the first principle of recovery is the empowerment of the survivor". She further suggests that the trauma victim is robbed of a sense of power and control. Therefore, the clinician must restore a sense of power, control, and safety in order to begin the healing process. Establishing safety begins by focusing on control of the body and gradually moving toward control of ones mind and environment.

To change the effects of PTSlaveryD we must first understand the cumulative toxic effects of the disorder and then enlighten the affected individuals to develop the necessary skills to be completely free. Therefore, since the disease began with the inception of slavery, it is relevant that we return to the thought process and the way of living of Black people during the pre-slavery period, a period of non-European influence.

Under the umbrella of PTSlaveryD comes a number of disorders and dysfunctions with symptoms that include:

o   Post Traumatic Stress Disorder: disorder related to a trauma
o   Economic Terror-Fear of losing job if speaking out against wrongs
o   Relational dysfunction-Emotional disconnect from Black women and Black Children
o   "Mentalcide:" mental homicide or suicide-through diet, lack of history, ignorance, and spiritual bond
o   Urban Psychosis-grossly disorganized/catatonic behavior, excessive hyper vigilance and paranoia
o   Avoidance of Education
o   Poor Physical Health-obesity, diabetic producing diet, high blood pressure
o   Lack of Higher income skills
o   Financial Illiteracy

o Employment Dysfunction: impaired ability to obtain/ keep a job
o Racial Identity Issues: self-hatred, skin color issues, impaired perception of what is being Black

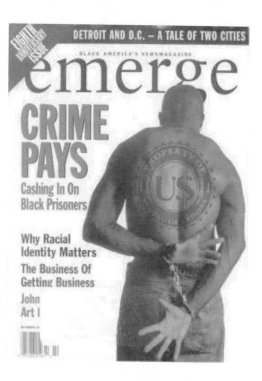

The following examples demonstrate behavioral manifestations directly related to PTSlaveryD.

1. On the plantation where Black people often worked seven days a week—sun up to sun down, two types of behavior emerged: a) Blacks who decided that they would gain the respect of the master by demonstrating that they were not lazy or ignorant worked hard to the point of killing themselves early. Today this behavior can be seen in many Blacks who work 45-80 hours

per week to be accepted as valued employees. They are often overlooked for promotions, and the first to be downsized which leads to high blood pressure and an early death; b) The second group of Black people slowed down the work pace by moving slowly and passive-aggressively because they rejected working hard for the master. Once again this form of resistance was functional during that period. Today, some Blacks avoid, reject, or refuse to work or seldom attempt to seek employment because they refuse to accept low wage jobs even though they lack the higher income skills.

Some Blacks turn to financial pathways that do not require legal training. They pursue illegal financial pathways that are easily accessible to them such as selling drugs, pimping, victimizing other victims, and using alcohol or drugs, which often leads them into the penal system and early death. This form of behavior plagues many Black males today and has resulted in high rates of incarceration and death nationwide. Too many Black people today are rejecting the path of education, legal corporate enterprise, and have opted for the quick money street trap.

2. During times of slavery, if a Black person was caught learning how to read he was killed. Often the tongue or eye of the slave attempting to read was removed to promote fear and terror in other Blacks thinking about learning the written language of the master. As a result, many Blacks never even attempted to read. Once again it was functional to avoid education because it resulted in extreme punishment. After slavery, many leaders such as Carter G. Woodson; Ida B. Wells; Thurgood Marshall; Dr. Martin L. King, Jr.; and Malcolm X educated themselves to help uplift other Black people. Those leaders were sent to jail,

assassinated or otherwise discredited in the news media sending a clear message to Blacks about their place in society. What has perpetuated this refusal to utilize education for upward mobility has been discrimination from jobs even when having the necessary education. Today many Black youth and adults still avoid education. Before integration Blacks attended schools with all Black teachers and they excelled in learning. Dropout, behavioral problems, and special education were virtually non-existent. When integration began, Black schools closed in favor of better-funded, predominantly white school systems. The culture shock has never been addressed and has resulted in high dropout rates, behavioral problems, and large number of referrals to *"Special Education."* Scholars argue the education Black students receive in urban communities is sub par in comparison to White middle class communities. Black students are "dumbed down" and are lacking in the necessary educational skills to participate in today's information economy. The below White middle class standard public school education Blacks often receive sets them up to not do well on tests like the SAT. At best, Black youth are educated just well enough to be low paid service workers and never be on the same level as many White middle class students.

Case Study: Tyrone is a 25-year-old Black male who dropped out of the 9th grade. He works odd jobs under the table when he finds employment. He mainly sleeps all day and hangs on the corner with his friends all night. He is not a drug dealer even though some of his friends sell drugs. They usually treat him to a beer and food each night and give him a few dollars to watch out for the police. Tyrone's mother recently died from a heart attack and he became homeless because he was unable to pay the rent. Tyrone explained that he hated school, because as a youth his teachers were all White females who would restrict him from asking questions when he needed help. In his experience, the classrooms were always over crowded and the teachers never had control of the students. Tyrone, became discouraged with school and stopped attending on a regular basis even though he was encouraged to get an education by his mother. Tyrone does not read well and he cannot spell, so when he attempted a GED program he dropped out because he was embarrassed about the skills he lacked. He never attempted to seek help because he felt that education was not an option for him. Tyrone often stated that he feels intimidated, anxious and tense when he attempts to seek education. These symptoms he felt while seeking education is the outcome of his being rejected and pushed away. Tyrone's father and grandfather were also school dropouts.

Case Study: Johnny is a 32-year-old Black male who has ten regular girlfriends and nine children. He has difficulty being committed to one relationship and being emotionally connected to his children. He grew up with six siblings who all had different fathers. Johnny never knew his father, who was murdered. However, his father also had several children by other women and never married. While doing research on his father, Johnny found that his father never had a relationship with *his* father (Johnny's grandfather). Through this discovery process Johnny began to understand that his emotional numbing came from PTSlavery D, and he was able to begin a process of recovery. Since then Johnny has become involved with his children on a regular basis and is now in one relationship.

Guidance with a holistic approach toward recovery from PTSlaveryD includes not only mental well-being, but physical and spiritual well being. Black people, as slaves, were treated like animals and given animal feed to live on. Due to a genius at adaptability they were able to turn animal feed into something delicious to eat although some of it was poor in nutrition and detrimental to the body. Over the years, Blacks have adapted those meals into what is called *soul food* today. As you know, Black people still eat soul food on a regular basis. This diet has a high amount of carbohydrates from white flour and white sugar resulting in high rates of diabetes. In addition, the meats in this diet are typically fried, which have resulted in an alarming rate of heart disease. In addition, Blacks often consume snacks that consist of artificial and processed foods that are high in sugar, salt and additives resulting in other health problems.

Case Study: Ms. Thomas is a 38 year-old Black female who originally came to therapy due to severe depression. In addition, she has diabetes, high blood pressure, high cholesterol, gout, and asthma. Her depression stemmed from all of her physical problems. She grew up in a loving *church family* where every night they had soul food including: fried chicken, fried pork chops or fried steak, macaroni salad, macaroni and cheese, potato salad, candied yams, collard greens, cakes, pies and Kool aid. She also ate three regular meals and two snacks daily and did no exercise, except for singing in the church choir. She was asked to bring in a chart of the ages and caused of death of people in her family. Once she realized that the people in her family were dying at an average age of fifty, compared to those with a healthy life expectancy of 75-85, Ms. Thomas began to change her diet. The changes were moderate at first baking and broiling meats instead of frying, replacing pork with turkey in collard greens, and green salad in place of potato and macaroni salad, unbleached wheat bread in place of white bread, and so on. Ms. Thomas. health improved tremendously over several months, especially when she included exercise in her life.

In the case study mentioned earlier, Ms Thomas was fortunate to stop the pattern of early death for herself—which had been the norm on both parents. sides of the family. Ms. Thomas. problem was rooted in PTSlaveryD because the food she ate was survival food passed on over the years from plantation living. Blacks have created an American culture in soul food, but must substitute certain ingredients that are detrimental to the body.

One symptom of PTSlaveryD that has not been directly addressed has to do with financial literacy. During slavery, only the master and his children were taught the benefits and importance of incorporation and financial literacy. Blacks, as mentioned earlier, were not even taught how to read. Black families have been led in so many different ways away from financial literacy, which continues to have a major impact on them as a group. For instance, Blacks are not involved in the major industries such as car manufacturing, furniture making, technology, food processing, oil refinery, material, textiles and other businesses as corporation owners and therefore are unable to hire their own in large numbers. Blacks are often encouraged by their family to go to school to get an education to get a good job and never to create one. Blacks at best are conditioned if they make it from the streets and traps of the system to be a house slave working for White corporation or business. The majority of Blacks consistently live paycheck to paycheck without savings and seldom supporting Black business because there are not many available. Scholars have studied this phenomenon sharing that the Asian dollar circulates through the Asian community 21 times before it leaves; the Jewish dollar circulates through the Jewish community 18 times; the Caucasian dollar circulates through the Caucasian community 12 times and the Black dollar circulates in the Black community approximately 2 times. On the plantation, during Apartheid/Jim Crow, during the Civil Rights Movement, and in the public schools today, Blacks have not been taught that it should be a top personal priority to raise their individual and collective financial literacy. As a result, even Blacks with education have an inadequate financial IQ. Blacks like Leon Sphinx, MC Hammer, Kareem Abdul Jabar, Lawrence Taylor, Hollywood Henderson, Ike Turner, Mike Tyson, and Sammy Davis Jr. have worked hard to make millions, and those same Blacks have lost their millions because of their low financial IQ.

Case study: Mr. Johnson a 47 seven year old Black computer engineer previously worked for a major semi-conductor company for 19 years. He was downsized and has been unable to find employment at the rate he has been accustomed. He lives in a home with a mortgage payment of $3,200.00 a month. He has used all his severance pay and is now using the money from his 401 K plan to pay his living expenses. He was depending on the company retirement plan to live on when he retired. Mr. Johnson had not developed other sources of revenue to protect himself financially. In addition, he was feeling depressed not just from losing his only financial resource (his job) but also from not working to develop his own business or financial shelter. He stated if he does not find employment he will be forced to live in *field slave* status soon. At one time, during the industrial revolution when manufacturing was prominent in America, one could get a job at the bottom of the company ladder and work their way to a retirement watch and a pension.

Today, due to the economy, companies are folding and merging so quickly that employees are being laid off by the thousands. Blacks have not been able to participate in the low end of the information economy to a large degree because as a group their collective skills are too low. The masses of Black people lack higher income skills. The corporate world is now doing business at the speed of thought and the Black community is just learning to read and do basic math.

A Curriculum Guide for PTSlaveryD

Omar G, Reid, Psy.D

If we are biologically stunted, nothing that we do to our minds will work. We have to prepare the body and the mind to take in knowledge.

I n this chapter we have designed a curriculum to work with the individual, the family, and groups who may be affected by PTSlaveryD. The curriculum is divided into a variety of lessons giving the therapist or facilitator a chance to integrate their experience and ideas into those lesson treatments. The material has been composed to allow a lesson to cover one session or several sessions. The main point is that the facilitator of the lessons understands how they want participants in the treatment to make progress toward recovery. In addition, the lessons have no time frames. The clinician can use the support lessons in any order or pace that is appropriate for the individual or group depending on the degree of PTSlavery D detoxification required. The curriculum is most effective for work with Black males. However, certain lessons can be modified or used for work with Black females.

Recovery from PTSlaveryD

The first step to recovery is to detoxify the mind of the affected individual before beginning the actual treatment. This is done by getting the individual to abstain from nicotine, alcohol, excessive caffeine (more than three cups of coffee daily), drugs, excessive dead foods, processed food, simple carbohydrates, processed carbohydrates, and artificial fluids. Participants should pick up the health book by Rector-Page (1998) which will give them extensive suggestion on developing their brain health and dealing with other medical issues they may be experiencing. The book list should be given to the participants in order for them to get the books to begin the detoxification process. Several videos should be ordered before beginning the program: *Is your food safe part 1 & 2* from CBS, 48 Hours (800) 338-4847, and *Dead Doctors Don't Lie* from 1-800-Wallach.

The next step involves the introduction and practice of meditation to help clear the mind of the daily stress and issues the individual may be experiencing during this time. The individual must on every meeting acknowledge ancestors through a moment of silence mentally tracing their existence back to the beginning of time on both sides of the family. Then the individual must be taught the history of which **they are** holistically; their story before slavery, during slavery, and during the current times. The individual must be shown how PTSlaveryD is manifested today in his or her behavior.

The final step is to develop new ways of existing in the world today utilizing the acquisition of knowledge and practices of Black people before the period of slavery. It is through this process that the individual or group can begin to rebuild the genius of the pyramids in the mind again.

> *   *The therapist who will use this curriculum must first go through the PTSlaveryD detoxification themselves to be effective in the delivery.*

ANTI-PTSlaveryD CURRICULUM

SUPPORT I: **INTRODUCTION TO SUPPORT GROUP**

GOAL: Introduction to the recovery process for PTSlaveryD, which will provide participants with the necessary skills to combat Post Traumatic Slavery Disorder

OBJECTIVES:

1. Introduce participants to the definition/process of PTSlaveryD and determine how they are affected;
2. To discuss the use of Genograms;
3. To increase the participants awareness of the holistic self (mind, body, spirit) and Nubian history;
4. To prepare the participants biologically, cognitively, and spiritually to begin the healing process from PTSLaveryD.

Rationale: The first lesson will focus on introducing the participant to the transformation process from PTSlaveryD to holistic freedom. The facilitator/therapist must give the participant the definition of PTSlaveryD and show how it is currently manifested now in the individual. The participant is given the procedure to a healthy recovery. The participant is then given a genogram form to complete on his or her own family. The genogram will be a work in progress over several lessons. It should include dates of birth, places of birth, where people grew up, why they moved, their talents, hobbies as well as date and cause of death. The facilitator/ therapist must emphasize that it is difficult to move forward mentally, physically, and spiritually if you do not know where you came from. The next and most important step is to show how the individual is a collective self. The individual is the product of all ancestors that came before his or her existence. Discuss the prognosis from PTSlavery D if the participant acquires the tools of self knowledge to break free from the disease.

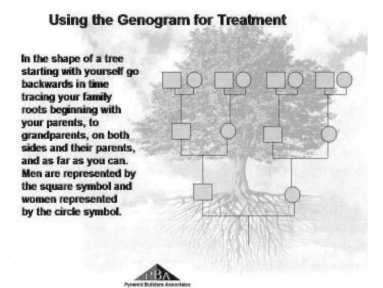

Using the Genogram for Treatment

In the shape of a tree starting with yourself go backwards in time tracing your family roots beginning with your parents, to grandparents, on both sides and their parents, and as far as you can. Men are represented by the square symbol and women represented by the circle symbol.

Pyramid Builders Associates

Above is an example genogram, the females are circles and the males are squares

Materials/Book:

- Akbar (1988) *Know Thy Self*
- Akbar (1996) *Breaking the Chain of Psychological Slavery*

SUPPORT II: **INTRODUCTION TO MENTAL SLAVERY**

GOAL: How we moved from pyramid builders to memory loss

OBJECTIVES:

1. The mind of Pyramid Builders
2. History of the Moors
3. Knowledge of the Willie Lynch method
4. Black labor/white wealth

Rationale: This lesson focuses on Black history before and during slavery. This may take several weeks. Emphasis is placed on the time of the Moors (Black Muslims) and the crusades. Williams's book (1975) and Sertima's books (1976, 1999) should be discussed in detail. Very few people know that Black people *ruled* Whites in Spain and Southern Portugal for over 700 years. The year the Black Moors were defeated was the same year that Christopher Columbus set sail for the Americas. The facilitator/therapist should ask the participant who was the Moor that the famous character Othello was based on? What were the crusades about? How much of the world did Blacks rule? What part of Africa has the most important architectural structures such as Pyramids? For homework, give the Willie Lynch article to all participants to read and encourage them to read it before the next session.

Books:

- Williams (1975) *Destruction of Black Civilization*
- Sertima (1976) *They Came Before Columbus*
- Sertima (1999) *Golden Age of the Moors*

Video:

- History Channel "The Pyramids."

Part 2

This second half should focus on the slave trade and the making of the slave.

The Willie lynch article should be discussed. Ask the participants what was their reaction to reading this article. Next show the movie Sankofa or Roots Part 1. After viewing the films have a discussion of what people thought, felt, and what thoughts have stayed with them after viewing the movie. For homework ask participants to bring in a list of how physical slavery exists today in the Sudan and what other forms of slavery exist: mental, subtle, subversive, subliminal; in other countries including the United States even though Black are assumed physically free. Have them give examples of how their mind, body, and spirit are enslaved today.

SUPPORT III: **THE CONTINUATION OF MENTAL SLAVERY**

GOAL: Introduction to the effects of PTSlaveryD today

OBJECTIVES:

1. Understanding capitalism,
2. The dumbing down process,
3. The impact of diet on physical, mental, and spiritual health.

Rationale: This session will cover how Blacks are mentally enslaved today. Get feedback from the participants on their list of how they are enslaved today. Emphasis should be on showing how capitalism is the driving force behind the dysfunction. Compare the conditions of Blacks during slavery with those who are illiterate, divided, and emotionally broken today. Ask participants which category of slavery they are being most affected by today. Ask them to explain Pros and Cons of that status in America today. The key here is to show them how they can better themselves, their family, and their community. Explain how capitalism is the driving force behind Black peoples dysfunction (Anderson, 1994). You can also use the first *Matrix* movie as an example of how most people are conditioned to not be fully awake.

Explain how being miseducated today affects Black people in general. Have participants discuss how they have been miseducated. Ask participants their reactions to the books Lies My Teacher Told Me (Loewen, 1996) and Mis-education of the Negro (Woodson, 1933). Show the movie Lean on Me. Discuss the condition and dress of the school when it was all White. Discuss how the school milieu changed when it became majority Black. Have participants explain what they thought about the movie as to being typical of many urban schools in predominantly Black communities.

Discuss how some Blacks are not only miseducated learners, but are miseducated about appropriate dress, health and diet. Have clients discuss why there is not a dress code in the public schools in the urban areas anymore. Ask them what are the advantages and disadvantages of dress codes. Have clients read Molloy's (1987) book *New Dress for Success*. Have all clients bring in a list of what they consume over the next few days. Have them bring in packages or containers of the items they consumed and read the labels as a group.

Books:

- Woodson (1933) *Mis-education of the Negro*
- Gatto (1992) *Dumbing us Down*
- Loewen (1996) *Lies My Teacher Told Me*
- Anderson (1994) *Black labor/ White Wealth*
- Molloy (1987) *New Dress for Success*
- Buchanan (2002) The Death of the West

- Film —"Lean on Me" and "The Matrix"

SUPPORT IV: **MENTALCIDE RECOVERY 1**

GOAL: The basic steps for the detoxification from PTSlaveryD

OBJECTIVES:

1. Getting the Mind in shape: Developing advanced meditation skills to introduce participants to Natural foods and build basic awareness of overall health. To give location and information on health stores to participants;
2. To introduce participants to herbs, Homeopathy, meditation, acupuncture, and the benefits from exercise, rest, and developing a connection with the environment.

Rationale: Have participants begin to practice meditation techniques 1 and 2. The purpose is to help them benefit from the biological and mental transformation, which occur during the next lessons. They should be encouraged to meditate on a regular basis.

Have participants list what they had for breakfast, lunch, and dinner over the last few days. Divide the list into two headings: dead foods and living foods. Put fruit, 100% fruit juice, water, veggies, fish (non-fried), nuts, and whole grains under living foods. Meats, processed foods (e.g., cookies, pies, chips, and candy) white bread, white rice, and artificial drinks under dead foods. Compare participant's level of dead foods vs. living foods. This session should be a lot of fun. Write down "you are what you eat" and begin asking participants what was the main thing they have come to realize about their food consumption? Ask them about what foods they find in Black neighborhoods they can never find in a wealthy White neighborhood? (A good example is Teeni drinks and Pork Rinds).

You can use the Malt liquor scene from the movie "Drop Squad." Explain the impact of diet. It will be good to give local or country statistics on health fatalities by race. Ask the question, "Why do Blacks have a higher proportion of deaths due to heart disease, diabetes, colon and prostate cancer compared to other ethnic groups?"

Have participants go back to their packages and read the number of carbohydrates they consumed daily and weekly. Explain the significance of measuring food in a diet of moderation i.e. 28gm. = 1oz and 16oz = 1lb, and 448gms will equal 1lb.

Show the video "Is Your Food Safe" part 1 by 48 hours (see addendum on how to order). Get the reaction from participants as to what they have learned about food and how it is processed. In addition, create new examples such as figuring out the amount of money that doctors and pharmaceutical companies would lose if everybody ate healthy. Order from CBS the 48 Hours documentary, "Is Your Food Safe" videos part 1 & 2 (800) 338-4847.

Give a list of health food stores close to the area. Arrange a field trip or encourage participants to visit. Ask participants "What neighborhoods most nature food stores are in?"

Have a speaker come to the group to discuss holistic medicine and information on what organic foods are. Introduce clients to soymilk and/or almond milk. Discuss setting a schedule for exercise, rest, and getting in touch with the environment (earth). Discuss the book "The Okinawa Program" extensively.

Books:

- Afrika (1994) *Nutricide*
- Rector-Page (1998) *Healthy Healing*
- Wilcox, et al (2001) *The Okinawa Program*

SUPPORT V: **MENTALCIDE RECOVERY 2**

GOAL: To enhance the participant's awareness regarding vitamins and minerals

OBJECTIVES:

1. To understand the effects of Vitamin/Mineral deficiencies;
2. To develop awareness regarding fungicides and pesticides;
3. To understand the impact of artificial ingredients, wax foods, and preservatives.

Rationale: Have participants listen to Dr. Joel Wallach's book, cassette or watch his video on "Dead Doctors Don't Lie". Get feedback from participants on how and why they have been misinformed about the health issues mentioned. Ask the question why and have them relate it to capitalism. As comedian Chris Rock stated "The money is in the treatment not the cure."

Show part 2 of 48 hours "Is your food safe". Have participants discuss what they have learned from the video? What can be done to protect themselves and their families? Encourage participants to use the food additives dictionary by Ruth Winters (1994) to look at dyes and artificial ingredients.

Book:

- Winter (1999) *Consumers Dictionary of Food Additives*

Video:
- Hours: "Is Your Food Safe" part 2
- Video or Cassette-"Dead Doctors Don't Lie"

SUPPORT VI: MENTALCIDE RECOVERY 3

GOAL: Raise understanding on the relationship between deviance and capitalism

OBJECTIVES:

1. To discuss the cost of crime,
2. To realize the Criminal Justice system exploits,
3. To learn about the CORI trap.

Rationale: This session is about the business of incarceration. However, you must first discuss the socialization process that gets most Black men caught up in the criminal justice system (Akil, 1996, Wilson, 1993). Discuss the cost to incarcerate an individual in your local prison system (information can be received from local state and federal penal system). HBO's "Thug Life in DC" is a great video to show including "Caught Up," "Menace to Society," "Belly," "Set It Off," and "Boys 'n the Hood". "The Education of Sonny Carson", and "Blue Hill Avenue".

The main thing to process is why so many Blacks follow deviant paths to become financially successful in America. The other key issue to bring up is once a person is in the system of criminal justice he is set up by the CORI process to have all positive avenues of social productivity blocked. Therefore, that person is almost forced back to a life of crime and further incarceration. Discuss how the criminal justice system is not a house of correction but a house of mis-education.

Books:

- Akil (1996) *From Niggas to Gods*
- Akbar (1996) *Breaking the Chains of Psychological Slavery*
- Wilson (1993) *Understanding Black Male Violence.*

Video: Bamboozled

SUPPORT VII: **PTSlaveryD RECOVERY 1**

GOAL: To enhance participant's awareness of Time Sickness

OBJECTIVES:

1. To introduce participants to self-care and organization of time,
2. To give participants information to begin the life transformation.

Rationale: The facilitator's goal is to get the participant to establish a spiritual power center which involves having an organized schedule for life planning and self-care. Begin quiet strategies on how to recover by first taking steps to put him or her in a calm space through the meditation. Discuss the problem of "Time Sickness." Time Sickness is when a person does not set aside enough time to take care of themselves mentally, physically or spiritually. It is called Time Sickness because the person afflicted is always on somebody else's time clock, and they can't seem to synchronize their own need for time in their schedule. Discuss how to bring balance in their life from the stressors of home life, family, and community.

Introduce participants to time-management, and the making of quiet time and exercise a must in their daily life-contemporary jazz; nature sounds, and guided imagery should be used. It is good to bring in tapes or CDs and let the participants discuss the body reaction from listening to the items. Have participants close their eyes and practice leaving the room they are in and traveling to a peaceful place in their mind.

Material/Books: contemporary Jazz artists

- Walter Beasley
- Paul Hardcastle
- Najee, etc.,
- Relaxation tapes

SUPPORT VIII: **PTSlaveryD RECOVERY 2**

GOAL: To introduce participants to the basics of financial intelligence

OBJECTIVE:

1. To introduce participants to basic financial literacy,
2. To introduce participants to short term strategies of raising their income potential.

Rationale: The facilitator can vary this lesson by the participant's financial intelligence. The main theme is that participants must set up an economic center for themselves by first beginning the basic financial step of paying themselves first and making their money work for them. Clients must read the works of Anderson (2001) and Kiyosaki (2000) to get an understanding of where they must be heading in their financial thinking.

The facilitator should compile a list of short-term job training programs ranging from one weekend to one year that will give participants the skills to get paid well above minimal wage. Short term training as a certified nursing assistant, surgical technician, radiological technician, LPN, EMT, cable installer, and so on should be provided for all participants. Individuals who require a GED program or an adult high school program should be given a list of community programs that provide the education they need. The emphasis should be on obtaining paper (Education/ skills) because without it the individual is doomed to field status as a slave. There should be a list of job training programs where a CORI will not impede progress. For people who have CORI issues this session should be very helpful.

Have participants view the movie *Disappearing Acts* and discuss what were the issues in the movie. Talk about the male character's main roadblock to obtaining steady income and becoming self-employed. This section is difficult and requires patience because most people in general regardless of race are conditioned to work on the plantation.

Books:

- Kiyosaki (2000) *Rich Dad, Poor Dad*
- Lynch & Rothchild (1995) *Learn to Earn*
- Anderson (2001) *PowerNomics*

Video
- "Disappearing Acts"

SUPPORT IX: **GOP ECONOMICS**

GOAL: To introduce participants to steps to get off plantations (GOP).

OBJECTIVE:

1. To discuss the Pros and Con of being self-employed,
2. To explore potential investment opportunities,
3. To discuss tax benefits from being self-employed.

Rationale: Self-employment strategies should be introduced to participants ranging from canteen trucks and transportation, to home repair. Adams Media Corporation has a CD called Adams Streetwise 500 businesses you can start. This CD could be used for illustrating some basic start-up businesses. Also, have local self-employed people come in and speak to the group about their business.

Have participants look into real estate as a business, http://www.realtor.com and other sites are available. Discuss the use of property managers and investing in other states like Japan and other foreign countries. Have speakers come in who are specialized in investing and business. You must emphasize the importance of preparing to retire.

Books:
- Jones (1996) *ADAMS Businesses You Can Start Almanac*

SUPPORT X: **PREVENTION OF PTSlaveryD RELAPSE**

GOAL: To introduce participants to steps to prevent PTSlaveryD relapse

OBJECTIVE:

1. Establishing a support group,
2. Relationship building.

Rationale: This lesson is to encourage support for developing the skills necessary to be in a relationship with our partners and with our children. Talk about how Black people lived in separate quarters on the plantation and how the breeding process caused a numbing effect emotionally for Black men. Discuss how Black men developed an inability to emotionally connect to our children and women. Through the genogram show how an inability to connect with a family life may have trickled down from generation to generation and may have been reintroduced or reinforced through their socialization process today.

Have participants discuss whether the relationships they have had with their mother and father are close or distant. Discuss what effect it had on their development. Have the men give account of the last time their father or stepfather hugged and kissed them. Assess the level of positive touch of the men by their fathers or stepfathers. Was it for support or for discipline only? This is important because men have to be taught how to love because for many years love resulted in retaliation and death on the plantation.

Discuss relationship practices and discipline practices during and after slavery and compare them with those experiences before slavery. The important point here is to show that certain relationship practices, sex practices, and discipline practices are a result of slavery. This lesson can be divided into several sessions focusing on how to love a woman, children, and self as well as how to forgive. For Black men in particular emphasis must be placed on how to develop qualities of humility and consistency, how to choose a mate, and how to water the plant of love in a relationship.

SUPPORT XI: **PREVENTION AND FAMILY**

GOAL: To assist the participant in establishing ways to protect the family system

OBJECTIVE:

1. The Family meeting,
2. Continuing the family Tree.

Rationale: This lesson is about maintaining positive communication between family members. Participants should be encouraged to have a weekly family meeting to discuss family business and plan family activities.

This family meeting should be consistent and non-challenging. It is about being heard and respected. This will contribute significantly in making the family unit cohesive. Ask participants if they had a family meeting in their life as a child in which everyone got together to discuss family issues and plan activities? What would that have done to improve communication within the family? How can you make this happen with your family? What day and time is good for the meeting?

The Family meeting is where the family history should be discussed. Keeping a family book and developing games for children to remember family history works well. The history should be updated regularly and vacations should be planned to visit relatives or burial sites of ancestors as well as the communities and places they lived.

- Video "Soul Food"

SUPPORT XII: **PREVENTION AND COMMUNITY**

GOAL: To establish ways to dissolve PTSlaveryD in the community at large

OBJECTIVES:

1. Discuss the creation of Charter schools,
2. Discuss the need for and use of Private Schools,
3. Discuss replacing lost African Archives of Egypt and Africa using the Black experience in America as a starting place to work back from.

Rationale: This lesson is to discuss the pros and cons of charter schools, private schools and vouchers. The facilitator should have people from charter schools and private schools come in to discuss their educational approach. Participants who are motivated should be encouraged to open up a charter or private school to educate their own children. Understand that Jewish people do not have Arabs teaching their children. Affluent Whites do not have the majority of Black people teaching their children. Therefore, if Blacks want a quality education so their children can open up corporations and improve the lives of Black people they must educate their own. Information on establishing charter and private schools should be given to participants.

The second part of this lesson is to strengthen the community by establishing archives of Black information. An archive is a collection of current and historic information on any given topic. An archive on Black people would help build a database of the vast range of experiences that Black have had throughout the centuries. In addition, collecting, reading and preserving this information and making it available for others will allow participants to begin to establish their own legacy as knowledge builders. This archive would be created and operated by individuals who have been detoxified from PTSlavery D and are far enough along in their process of recovery. An individual, family, or group would enter the archive and would be given step by step instructions on why the information is important, how to obtain the information in a specific order, and how to apply the information for their personal, family, and community growth.

Pyramid Builders Reading and Reference List

1. Afrika, L.O. (1994). Nutricide: The nutrional destruction of the Black race. Beaufort, SC, Golden Seal Press.
2. Akbar, N. (1988). Know Thy Self. Tallahassee, FL: Mind Productions & Associates.
3. Akbar, N. (1991). Visions for Black Men. Tallahassee, FL: Mind Productions & Associates.
4. Akbar, N. (1996). Breaking the Chains of Psychological Slavery. Tallahassee, FL: Mind Productions & Associates.
5. Akil, C. (1996). From Niggas to Gods Part One & Two. Atlanta, GA. Nia Communication/Press.
6. American Psychiatric Association: *Diagnostic and Statistical Manual of Mental Disorders,* Fourth Edition. Washington, DC, American Psychiatric Association, 1994.
7. Anderson, C. (1994). Black Labor, White Wealth: The search for power and economic justice. New York, NY. PowerNomics Corp of America.
8. Anderson, C. (2001). PowerNomics: The National plan to empower Black America. New York, NY. Powernomics Corp of America.
9. Bogle, D. (1989). Toms, Coon, Mulattoes, Mammies, & Bucks. New York, NY. The Continuum Publishing Company.
10. Brown, Tony. (1995). Black Lies, White Lies: The truth according to Tony Brown. New York, NY: William Morrow and Company, Inc.

11. Buchanan, Patrick. (2002). The Death of the West. New York, NY: St. Martin's Press.
12. Carlson. E. (1997). Trauma Assessments: A Clinician's Guide. New York, NY. The Guilford Press.
13. Cress-Welsing, F. (1991). The Isis Papers. Chicago, IL: Third World Press.
14. Cross, W. (1991). Shades of Black. Philadelphia, PA. Temple University Press.
15. Danieli, Yael. (Ed). (1998). *International Handbook of Multigenerational Legacies of Trauma.* New York, NY. Plenum Press.
16. Department of Education.: *Department of Education Federal Register,* Washington, DC Press, Department of Education, 1999.
17. Feelings, T. (1995). The Middle Passage. New York, NY. Dial Books.
18. Gatto, J. (1992). Dumbing Us Down: The Hidden Curriculum of Compulsory Schooling. Gabriola, BC, New Society Publishers.
19. Graham, L.O. (1999). Our Kind of People. New York, NY. Harper Collins Publishing, Inc.
20. Herman, J. (1992). Trauma and Recovery. New York, NAY. Basic Books.
21. James, G. (1992). Stolen Legacy: Greek philosophy is stolen Egyptian philosophy. Trenton NJ, First Africa World Press, Inc.
22. Jones, K. (1996). ADAMS Businesses You Can Start Almanac. Adams Media Corporation.
23. Kiyosaki, R. (2000). Rich Dad, Poor Dad: What the rich teach their kids about money. New York, NY. Warner Books, Inc,.
24. Kunjufu, K. (1984). Developing Positive Self-Images & Discipline in Black Children. Chicago, IL. African-American Images.
25. Kunjufu, K. (1991). Black Economics: Solutions for economic and community empowerment. Chicago, IL. African-American Images.

26. Kunjufu, K. (1995). Countering the Conspiracy to Destroy Black Boys: Volumes 1-4. Chicago, IL. African-American Images.

27. Loewen, James. (1996) Lies My Teacher Told Me: Everything your American history textbook got wrong. New York, NY. Simon & Schuster Trade.

28. Lushena Books. (1999). Willie Lynch letter and the Making of a Slave.

29. Lynch, P. & Rothchild, J. (1995). Learn to Earn: A beginnerís guide to the basics of investing. New York, NY, Simon & Schuster.

30. Molloy, J. (1987). New Dress for Success. New York, NY, Warner Books, Inc.

31. Rector-Page, L. (1998). Healthy Healing. Healthy Healing Publications

32. Sertima, Ivan. (1976). They Came Before Columbus. Random House, Inc.

33. Sertima, Ivan (1999). Golden Age of the Moor. New Brunswick, NJ. Transaction Publishers.

34. Wallach, Joel. (1999). Dead Doctors Donít Lie. Legacy Communications.

35. Willcox, B., Willcox. D.C., & Suzuki, M. (2001). The Okinawa Program. New York, NY. Clarkson Potter.

36. Williams, Chancellor (1975). The Destruction of Black Civilization, Chicago, IL. Third World Press.

37. Wilson, Amos. (1993). Understanding violence in Black males: Its Remediation and Prevention. New York, NY. Afrikan World InfoSystems.

38. Winter, Ruth. (1999). A Consumerís Dictionary of Food Additives. Three River Press.

39. Woodson, C. (1933). The Mis-Education of The Negro. United Brothers Communication Systems/ KHA Books 26070 Barhamshill Rd. Drewryville V.A. 23844